FISHING FOR MORE

A Memoir

BRETT BLOEMENDAAL

FISHING FOR MORE: A MEMOIR

First Printing 2021
Copyright 2021 Brett Bloemendaal
Bloemendaalfishing.com
Granger, IA 50109

This is a work of nonfiction. Some of the character names have been changed, though they are real people, not composites.

Cover Design By: Laura Boyle
Cover Image By: Randy Belisle
Edited By: Shire Brown

ISBN: 978-1-7368465-2-0 (hardback)
ISBN: 978-1-7368465-1-3 (paperback)
ISBN: 978-1-7368465-0-6 (e-book)

To everyone who supported my journey in their own special way.

INTRODUCTION

Think back—way back—to a time when you were a little person gliding weightlessly across the grass, then maybe even the sandy shores of a river, lake, or the ocean. Perhaps you can smell the sun baking on your skin or the dew evaporating off the ground and the trees, pulling all the scents of nature toward your nose in a cocktail of life's flavors. You gather rocks for your pockets, or pick dandelions, maybe even cast a line into the water to see if something will bite. Or just watch fish play at the surface.

Sit with it for a while and notice how you feel. What comes back to you? Are they things you forgot but now seem so familiar? It's you, unfiltered and pure. You're not acting or playing a part. You aren't working to meet expectations; you're just being you. Do things seem different? Can you feel priorities shifting within you? Suddenly what seemed set in stone may become surprisingly malleable, even after all those years and all those walks down well-worn paths.

Now, can you meld that unbridled, childlike adventure with the knowledge and resources of your adult self? We often say "If only I knew now what I knew then." Well, all those past selves are still part of you in spirit. You know what you know now, and part of you is still who you were then. At any moment you could choose to change your path with your next step, whether a major overhaul or a subtle shift, tweaking your way to a better tomorrow. As you stare at the water, the sun warm on your back, the horizon sprawling endlessly in front of you—and knowing your adult self can now take the reins of its own destiny—what do you want to do? Is there a fresh path calling your name?

I was in my mid-30s when I first started questioning my own worn out yet comfortable path, so perhaps I was due for an existential crisis. Or it's possible it just took that many years for me to get a good enough handle on my own self to know what I really wanted out of life and/or grow a pair large enough to make it happen. If the life-altering decisions that prompted the writing of this book didn't get me all the way there—and no one ever gets all the way—the writing process itself did the rest of the heavy lifting.

After setting out on this endeavor, I remember getting to a point where I had maybe seventy pages and thinking to myself "where the hell is the rest of this book?" As I read back through the existing material, I realized I wasn't going deep enough. I have been accused of being overly wordy before, but sometimes my words were more of a creative distraction from the truth. I had yet to meet my catalyst for the genuine introspection worthy of a good memoir.

Even then, it only got me through those seventy pages, and again I felt stuck, as I had in life, until something clicked. I began to notice scenes that I had glossed over or outright skipped because they made me uncomfortable. Then it dawned on me that those were the very things I need to address and really delve into because they were, in fact, the meat of the story. If those memories weren't fully shown and unpacked, I suspect you would question yourself over and over again as to why the hell you were even bothering. It became my intention to leave no reader hungry.

This isn't to say that I got everything right. Though I tried my best, and often tout my self-proclaimed eidetic memory to my friends and family, surely there are things I missed or got wrong, but not intentionally. In fact, this obsession with being "right" also paralyzed me and held me up in the middle of the project until I allowed myself to forget being *right* and just *write*. After all, that's what rough drafts are for. Still, through meticulous rewriting and help from some wonderful critique partners and editors, I believe my truth is as accurate as I can portray it from my present-day perspective.

The other funny thing about memory, besides it's somewhat fluid nature over time, is how much of it is actually embedded in brain tissues of which we are completely unaware on a day-to-day basis. There were scenes that I felt belonged in this book, but when I sat down to write them, I felt as though I didn't remember anything substantive enough for anyone to care. How can I show the reader something I can't conjure up myself? The only thing I remember about that day is the smell of the rain-soaked sand on the shores of the river mixing with my sunbaked skin and a hint of Coppertone . . . Oh! There it is! And then I was off to the races. Memory conjures itself and all its friends like a pied piper once it finds the right note to start the song.

There is a fine line between reinventing yourself and simply remembering yourself, if there is a line at all. Reading back through the portions about my childhood, my current life path seems inevitable, but it took one hell of a detour to get there. I suppose that's what made the story worthy of a full-length memoir, one that I didn't set out to write so much as it set out to *right* me.

This role reversal made for a satisfying result for me and, hopefully, you as a reader. Instead of starting out wanting to write a book and then thinking "Okay, now what do I write? What would be a good story?" this one more or less channeled me as a way out into the world. It floated up into my consciousness and demanded to be heard. Had I tried to suppress it, I suspect I would have developed sleepwalking insomnia and dictated the entire thing to my computer in the wee hours of every night.

The book became a borderline obsession, which is usually the state from which I work best, so long as I can navigate it carefully. There's a fine line between harnessing that intensity for good and falling into the abyss. I shook hands with the darkness a few times throughout the process. She remembered me, but this time I told her unfortunately I wasn't able to stay. I had other places to be.

In the pages that follow, I invite you to join me as I reconnect with my young, adventurous fisherman-self, remember how I lost him, and discover what it meant to find him back. My guess is that along the way it will stir up something you have been aching to reconnect with as well. I thought my little dude just wanted to catch fish, but it turns out he was searching for much more than that.

Me with my first known fish
catch on record.

ZOMBIE

IF THIS IS what we call progress, maybe I don't want to be part of it. We originally built corporations to make *our* lives better, and now we seem to exist to make their bottom lines bigger. Speaking of which, my bottom line is decomposing in this chair, and my sense of purpose is melting like the polar ice caps—all of it attributable to a perverted view of success. My eyes are tired of these screens. My brain longs for novel stimulation. And my soul knows the paycheck isn't fixing any of it.

When I pursued a desk-job career path, I thought I was saving myself from the hardships of physical labor. Ironically, my body is now suffering from a lack thereof. Normally, I love irony. I can often see the humor in it all, or at least I could in the past. But I don't laugh much anymore. My body seems to know only pain, and my mind seems to know only numbness. Everything is exhausting. Nothing seems to matter. Why get exhausted over nothing?

It makes zero sense to feel exhausted after a day of nothing, but I do. To anyone challenging the idea, I'd ask you to remember the last time you were in a doctor's office and, forty-five minutes past your scheduled appointment, you continue to wait, rereading *People* magazine a third time for no purpose other than to kill the time. Then add another seven hours, every day. Lack of purpose and accomplishment is as exhausting as running a marathon, even if it is in a totally different way. So, in the spirit of mental health, I need a five-minute break. Perusing some fish pictures seems like a good escape right now.

After a few swipes through my collection, I find a shot of myself holding up two twenty-four-inch walleyes I caught last year while fishing at Devil's Lake, North Dakota. The fish were wonderfully photogenic, but I hold them at an awkward angle and their gills are flared at the camera, cheapening the photo. I should have known better, but I was excited and distracted.

Next is a picture of Dad with a tiny walleye on his line barely bigger than the lure he's used to catch it. The photo captures him grinning widely as he laughs at his little specimen a moment before becoming agitated when he discovered I wasn't merely observing but was actually immortalizing the moment.

"Don't you post that picture on Facebook!"

I don't know if he was more upset about the size of the fish or the view of his shirtless belly. I didn't care—the sight was too good to keep to ourselves. I've always felt the best picture-worthy fish are the biggest and the smallest, and I'm not all about window dressing. That tiny little cigar-shaped walleye was as much a part of our true experience as the big ones were.

A few swipes later, I stop to admire another one of my favorite pictures. Dad is holding the biggest catch of the trip, a twenty-six-inch, broad-shouldered tank of a walleye speckled in glorious green and yellow hues with pristine marble eyes. Tired from the fight, it hangs vertically from Dad's index finger like a wet leather jacket drying on a coat hanger. Dad's veteran instincts orient the full side of the fish toward the camera perfectly. His smile shows that old fire again.

He had caught that fish around 9:30 a.m. the first day of our maiden voyage to Devils Lake. The destination wasn't even our first choice; it was an audible we called at the last minute when our usual haunts in South Dakota were predicted to experience

100-degree heat waves that would no doubt grind fishing to a halt. The best way to escape the heat is to drive north. And that's how I found myself fishing in North Dakota for the first time.

"This thing's pulling so hard, Brett. I'm worried it's gonna break me off."

"Here, I'll slow the boat down a bit."

When it surfaced, I froze for what seemed an eternity, completely in awe of the specimen, then quickly shook myself awake and swooped it up with the landing net. Still full of six or seven pounds of walleye, I set the net down on the floor of the boat, expecting Dad to grab his fish. He grabbed me in a huge bear hug instead as we both shouted like giddy school kids.

"That just made the trip right there!" he said shortly after releasing me. Then I snapped a picture for which he was more than proud to pose. Then he released the fish as well. You have to let 'em go to let 'em grow.

These fishing vacations once served as a nice break, leaving me reenergized and ready to play investment analyst. Now they remind me of what else I could be doing. It's not just that I miss the water now as I sit at my desk but that I have a powerful sense I ought to be there instead. I need to be there. I belong there. I miss the feeling of belonging.

We don't all get what we want, though. Following your passion is the territory of the delusional and the irresponsible, not to mention embarrassingly cliché. It's okay. I'm responsible. I'll be fine. I'm fine. I close the photo app and place my phone upside down on my desk.

There must be a hundred people on this floor, and not one of them is speaking, not to each other, not on the phone, not a word. Nobody is moving either. Every half-dead pair of eyes is fixed on a screen of some form or another. Doesn't anyone have to go to a meeting? Is anybody going to eat a meal? Does anyone have to go to the bathroom? I am growing more and more antsy just watching other people.

The cold, dull overhead lighting glows gray like the aura of a quiet, soulless spirit. Reflecting off sterile white walls, it steadily depletes any vigor I have left and leaves my eyes dry and tired, much like hours of meandering through endless aisles of warehouse stores searching for the best buys on generic mayo and saltine crackers. It's enough to sustain life but does little to help it thrive. I miss the warm, vibrant sun.

I have about eight things I could be doing right now, but each one of them depends upon somebody else. I suppose I could send another round of follow-up emails, but that starts to get bothersome for both parties after a while. Still, it seems tomorrow's checklist will bear an uncomfortable resemblance to yesterday's save for a few letters retraced in pen for clarity, one "followed up again" notation with a current date, and a couple doodles of lake maps and golf hole designs.

No offense to my coworkers. My higher mind understands this is the reality of Corporate America. Right now my lizard brain would rather selfishly throw a Nerf football at the back of a few people's heads to get their attention and charitably knock their zombie asses back into consciousness. I resent the fact that "playfulness" has been placed under the unspoken *unprofessional* column. I don't want to be professional; I want to be real. Real can still be productive. Real can probably be more productive.

I have to figure out a way to make this better. Perhaps I'm not giving it enough effort. Or maybe I haven't effectively communicated my career desires to those around me. What else am I going to do? I have a dozen years of experience and a reputation now built on top of a double-major undergraduate degree in economics and finance as well as my Certificate in Investment Performance Measurement (CIPM), my world's equivalent to an accountant's CPA designation.

I was top of my class in economics and close to it in finance. I started fast in the investment world, earning bonuses, awards, multiple promotions, and a healthy salary. Taking inventory of my last few years, though, I don't even have enough to fill a sentence worth of any reader's time.

Feeling defeated, I need an excuse to leave my seat. Maybe I will go to the restroom again despite how it must confuse my mostly empty bladder. After twenty-seven steps and a right turn, I see someone I know in the hallway. His eyes are fixed on the floor, and he avoids eye contact, probably not out of malice but perhaps apathy.

I give him a chance, greeting him with a "Hey! How's it goin', man?"

Nothing but silence as he keeps his gaze on the floor and then on his phone as he continues to walk toward wherever it is he needs to be.

After visiting the bathroom and doing a lap around the floor, I return back to my desk. Perhaps I will start one of these projects, and when I do get some feedback, I can update it appropriately. Mentally this feels like a waste of time, but so is not doing anything. I can feel the tension creep into my shoulders, crawling from my fingers through my forearms all the way up to my head. My muscles begin to clench, compressing my joints, which pop audibly as air and fluid are squeezed from between them. It is almost as if I am being cryogenically frozen here in this supposedly ergonomic office chair, an oxymoron, especially for someone of my stature. I already spend forty hours a week sitting here. Why not make it an eternity?

The muscles in my chest and ribs tense further as they become even more exhausted. When I try to move, they seem to spasm against me, holding my gaze straight as if they've been overridden by malware, a computer virus that has mutated and learned to jump to humans. The tighter they get, the more effort it takes to breathe, my own muscle fibers turning against me like a pet python gone rogue. I no longer have control.

Ding. I receive an email bringing hope of relief, but as I read, I realize it is not related to any one of the eight things I was hoping for. The words are stunningly harsh; I can't imagine this person saying anything of the sort face-to-face. The distance of email loosens human inhibitions and allows one's venom to flow freely from fingers to keyboard, at which point it leaps electronically through my screen and into me.

My heart starts to beat uncontrollably. My face gets flushed with blood one moment, then it all seems to dump straight down to the floor the next. Everything gets cold. My field of vision starts to shrink. I'm not sure if I'm going to stay with it. I need to get up and go somewhere, but my options are limited.

As I walk toward the elevator, I beg my nervous system to keep me online. Thankfully, no one is in the elevator when the door opens. There is a conference room a couple of floors up, little used and equipped with a padded bench. I remember well because I've used it before upon noticing the onset of an episode —anxiety attacks, according to my doctor.

As I round the corner out of the elevator bay, I notice another coworker, and this one actually acknowledges my existence. Now it is I who have somewhere to be—somewhere to be in a hurry!—and I make quick, drive-by small talk without breaking stride, loathing my hypocritical self as I walk. I reach the conference room and am extremely relieved the lights are dark. I go in, close the door, and lie down on the bench, staring at the ceiling, trying to remember the breathing exercises.

It takes about twenty minutes for this attack to blow over and my racing heart to relax. I'm relieved no one ever entered the room, the possibility of which had worried me more and more with the sound of each passing person. I feel able to stand and walk back to the elevators again.

As I move past all of the bodies on the way back to my desk, little has changed. I get the sense that I could cartwheel naked all the way back without anyone noticing, if I even knew how to do one, that is. Is this what the matrix looks like? I am pretty sure these are real people, the people I know and work with, but for the first time, watching them all from this perspective, a touch of doubt starts to creep into my mind.

Are they hurting too? Physically or mentally? Emotionally? Do they want to scream as much as I do? Or are they cool with this? Is this just normal? Is this the way we operate, everything either in our heads or delivered electronically through keystrokes? Surely no little kid grew up dreaming of this thirty years ago.

I had originally been flushed with embarrassment over this runaway train that has become my nervous system, self-conscious about my retreat to a dark conference room, but I'm learning none of it is on anyone's radar. Case in point, about a week ago I had a similar attack. That time, however, I couldn't make it to the elevator. In that attack I got out of my seat, knelt down on the floor, and rolled over onto my back. I probably lay there for about two full minutes. Eventually, it passed. I stood up, opened my eyes, and looked around. It was as if nothing had even happened. No one stopped working. No one got out of their seat to come see what was happening. No one even shifted their gaze from their computer screen or offered a courtesy "Are you okay?" I just sat down and went back to work.

"What time is it?" I think to myself. The clock tells me 2:17 p.m. I've made an executive decision: I'm leaving early today.

It seems unusual to think a person ought to make less money, but seriously, what are they paying me for? I suppose someone else may see this as a perfect, cushy job. I should just shut up and keep cashing the paychecks, but my heart and my gut don't see it that way. They just see time squandered. Nothing getting done. No reason to be here. I don't want to be here.

It starts to rain outside. I can hear the drops hit the window near my desk. The sound triggers memories of a rainstorm at my first childhood home over thirty years ago. My parents were out that day, and I was spending it with Helen.

Helen was a wonderfully sweet old lady. She is my memory's first-known caretaker outside of my family, my first "babysitter," if you will. I'm not sure how we humans came up with the term "babysitter." Taken literally, there's no way most parents would pay for such a service, and the employee would likely end up in jail or escorted out by the Department of Human Services. But Helen never once sat on me.

Raising your first child certainly can't be easy, but my parents must have done a few things right. Enlisting Helen to take care of me ranks toward the top. She was an authority figure, but always in the kindest way, getting you to do what you ought to without overt aggression or "making you hate her," to use a bit of my childhood parlance.

She was the opposite of my subsequent babysitter, Ruth, who once yelled at me for throwing up on the carpet and was absolutely not fond of me playing with my stuffed animals all morning when there were apparently more productive things for a four-year-old to be accomplishing. I have no idea what Ruth's problem was, but she had one. Her best attribute was her ability to make me like Helen more.

After a good rain shower, Helen used to take me "fishing." The rainwater would run through the sides of the streets into the storm drains, and worms coming out of their holes to explore the newly-saturated world would inevitably wash down these little roadside streams. It seems ironic that worms were actually our target species rather than bait, but the purest of fisher people must start first with learning to catch their bait. Also, I was two, and Helen was just trying to keep me entertained.

I've always loved the fishy smell when it rains. I'm not totally sure what makes it smell that way. Clearly there aren't fish falling in the raindrops. I wondered if it was perhaps the slime of the worms themselves as they came out to play. I've also heard it may be the rainwater mixing with the oils of various plants and trees.

She would help me hunt in the backyard for the appropriate sticks to serve as poles, tie on some kite string or knitting yarn, fashion a hook out of a paperclip, and off we'd go. We sat on the curb waiting for worms to wash downstream to us and dropped our lines in an attempt to catch them. I honestly don't remember if we were ever successful. I wouldn't be surprised if I eventually just grabbed them with my hands, a tactic I still think about at times when walleyes are being stubborn, though they'd be hard to catch this way too.

I sorely want to be fishing right now. I imagine my dad does too. I know he does. I wish I could just call him up and tell him I'll be there in four hours, boat in tow, for another epic Bloemendaal fishing adventure.

Bloemendaal isn't just our family surname; it's also a place I've never visited, a municipality of Holland with Bloemendaal Beach functioning as a gateway to the North Sea. Wooden shoes, windmills, and tulips are relics of a Dutch heritage I never truly lived beyond festivals, parades, old family photos, and occasionally stumbling around in a pair of my grandma's old, clip-cloppy footwear as a toddler. Our relationship with water, however, flows in the blood and cannot be ignored. Without water, I am but a hunk of inanimate meat.

Most all of our Bloemendaal family tree has some affinity for the beauty of water and the creatures swimming within. My uncle Bevan doesn't fish but was so drawn to water he eventually realized his dream of owning property on the Atlantic through years of work and strategic planning. Grandpa and Grandma would take me and my younger brother, Brandon, fishing at local bass and bluegill ponds near their home. Dad said he heard that old saying "Wind from the west, fishing's the best . . . wind from the east, you catch the least" from his grandpa.

I look out my office window at the flag across the street. There is a nice, steady breeze blowing out of the west today, just enough for a good chop, not too much to be obstructive to a fisherman's efforts.

In my most formative years, my dad was an idol to me. He was bigger than life, indestructible, unstoppable, and formidable. He sported a badass, Jean-Claude Van Damme from *Hard Target* permed mullet and an earring to go along with his leather jacket during most of my childhood. It was a look he used during his undercover law enforcement days, but he could've pulled it off without any excuse. Proudest and most loving father of children I've ever known, but if you messed up, he was intimidating as hell.

I remember watching the *Ghostbusters* movie one afternoon while Dad was at work. I was already a Bill Murray fan at age four (and a Johnny Carson fan, for that matter, much to the chagrin of my desperate mother trying to put her child to bed at a decent time). When Dad came back after his shift, I reenacted the scene after the 'busters catch their first ghost. I looked at my father and shouted, "We came, we saw, we kicked ass!" I had no idea that what I had said was frowned upon coming from a young child's mouth, but two seconds of death stare had me throwing my blanket back over my head and running into my bedroom.

He'd give you the shirt off his back, drive through a snow storm to pick you up, and lift you up on his shoulders to see over the other adults. He also fished. Really well. He took us to the local ponds and rivers to shore fish, then later to the lakes in his boat. Eventually, when we were ready, he'd take us to his most revered fishery, the Missouri River. You could have offered me a hundred dollars back then to fish in someone else's boat other than Dad's, and I would have emphatically told you where you could stick your money. My dad simply was fishing to me.

I look at the clock again. It's 3:45 p.m. Close enough. I turn off my computer, grab my bag, push in my chair, and walk toward the elevators. No one says anything. Most don't look up from their screens. One nods his head.

During my elevator ride, I attempt to release all my frustrations and reset for tomorrow by having a bunch of uncomfortable mock conversations in my head. It's a very ineffective "trick" I've taught myself to make it through another day, but even while I'm doing it, I know I'm deceiving myself. I try to reason with myself that it's going to be different tomorrow, that something *might* change even though deep down I know it won't, not if I don't.

As I leave the building and walk toward the parking garage, the rain has stopped, leaving that fishy after smell. If this one cog didn't show up tomorrow, would the machine even notice? Regardless, what am I going to do? Just quit and go fish every day? Of course not. I'm not delusional. I'm responsible.

THE BIG WATER

THE FIRST TIME I saw the ocean was just over a decade into my young life. If this seems like a long time, one must remember living in Iowa puts you about as far away from either coast as possible. Nevertheless, it was a trip to New York to visit Uncle Bevan which gave me my first opportunity. The city was great for a while, seeing the buildings, the people—so many people—but if I could've spent every day at the ocean, I probably would have, boogieboard skin rashes be damned.

I always loved playing at "the beach" in general terms—and, up to this point in my life, always freshwater terms—but this was something altogether different. It was mind-boggling to look out to the horizon and this time not be able to see land on the other side. Watching the waves continue pushing into shore whether the wind blew or not made it quite mysterious and enchanting. It's often true the bigger the environment the bigger the animals inhabiting it, and I couldn't help but wonder how big the fish were.

Fishing the small ponds, lakes, and rivers near my home was certainly more fun than algebra homework, but I always wanted more. Besides, my dad always got to go to the "big water," as I called it, the reservoirs of the Missouri River. They weren't ocean big, but from a walleye-fishing perspective, especially from my perspective as a young boy, they were huge. At around age twelve, and with a few years of swimming lessons under my belt (Dad's requirement), I finally got that chance. Just me, Dad, and the big water. And my Uncle Brian. Part of me was jealous sharing the experience, but the other part had heard of his legendary snoring capabilities.

Brian is not a Bloemendaal; he belongs to my grandma's side of the family, one of her brothers, but he's also afflicted with the fishing bug. My dad always calls him "Red," for reasons I don't understand. My best guess is that he used to have red hair, but I've only ever known him with silvery grayish-brown hair, although I seem to remember a little reddish tint in his Teddy Roosevelt mustache once upon a time, the one he huffs through when he breaths and speaks.

In fact, if I were put on the spot to give him a nickname, it would be Teddy. Beyond the mustache, he also has the hair, the glasses, the build, and seems as though he might be perfectly comfortable with his pipe and a bottle of whiskey at a saloon in the early 1900s or gallivanting around the country with the other Rough Riders. He told me he was on the weightlifting team in college, which immediately ginned up thoughts of him in one of those turn-of-the-century, black-and-white photos of two men in a boxing match. At the same time, though, he seems much too laid-back for a fighter.

All weekend long, the song "Red Red Wine" from UB40 was stuck in my head, and how could it not be? In that day and age, most everyone was stuck listening to Top 40 hits on the radio during car rides, if they were lucky enough to even get a signal at all, especially during road trips through South Dakota. Unless you adore sprawling fields of corn and wheat, until reaching the hills along the river, the most entertaining sights along the way are a handful of signs reminding you how many miles you have left to Wall Drug.

The X-Files had also just come on air and nestled itself into my consciousness as not only one of my favorite shows but also a primary source of evening nightmares. That was, at least, until Teddy's log sawing cut off my sleepy dream signals like a bolt of lightning hitting a television antenna. The snoring was much worse than TV static—it was one nightmare or another. Thankfully, at that age I was much more resilient to a lack of sleep.

Our watery playground for this trip was the walleye factory of Lake Francis Case, one of the "big water" Missouri River reservoirs but smaller than big brother and sister Oahe and Sakakawea upstream. Up even further is the first reservoir in the system, Fort Peck Lake. Generally, whether by coincidence or design, the reservoirs tend to get bigger in size as you travel upstream north and west from Gavin's Point Dam near Yankton, South Dakota, all the way up to Fort Peck, Montana. The fact that a part of a river can be called a lake was confusing as hell to me as a child.

As the dams were added along the river to help with flood control (with the side benefit of providing hydroelectric power) the land above each dam was flooded into massive "impoundments" or "reservoirs." Immediately above each dam, the water is wide across and will appear still like a lake. Immediately below, the water will run quickly through a narrow spillway with noticeable current and look more like a river. As you follow downstream from one dam to the next, the current will slowly fade away, bleeding into the next "lake" as it gets wider and wider. It's a rather arbitrary line as to where the river stops and the next lake starts.

We stayed and fished near the town of Chamberlain, South Dakota, the only location on this section of Lake Francis Case where you can find food, gas, and lodging for many miles in either direction. It is also home to the popular Al's Oasis, famous for hot apple pie à la mode with cinnamon ice cream and its all-week prime rib special.

That first particular trip, however, we ate most of our dinners at A&W, as I recall, since it was a short walk from our luxurious lodgings at the Super 8 Motel. At least they had those novel little telephones with which to place your order and my favorite kind of root beer. I can still smell the fryer grease in my nose and feel the sensation of soda bubbles popping up in my nostrils as I sipped from that famous glass mug, the one which made me feel just mature enough for a fishing trip with the men.

One of those nights, either the first or the second, we walked into A&W under clear skies and walked out to find tall dark clouds quickly climbing over the bluffs on the other side of the river. After walking back to the motel, we got word either from our TV or another guest that there was a tornado in the area. As the clouds started to swallow the sky above our motel and the swirling winds threw dust in our faces, Dad ran over to cover the boat.

"Run back inside the motel, Brett," he yelled on the move. I snuck inside the glass door, shut it behind me, and watched him work as heavy rain started pelting the gravel as well as my dad. I think at one point the rain turned to hail, either before or after he got back inside.

The storm passed quickly, and we never did see a tornado, but the straight-line winds had stirred up the place.

"This might turn the fish off tomorrow," Dad said.

"Why?" I feel I owe Dad a nickel for every time I asked that, but I don't have the funds to cover.

"All that rain and lightning can spook 'em. I just don't want you to get your little hopes up."

He was always trying to protect me from disappointment. Nevertheless, I would always wake up excited and optimistic.

For breakfast we would take to the café at the marina before launching. Any good fisherman knows you have to stuff yourself as full of French toast, bacon, and eggs as you can if you intend to catch any fish out on the water. As a growing boy, I pretty much always held up my end of the bargain and got my (Dad's) money's worth. Once that last delicious bite went down the hatch, and after a brief perusal of the trinkets at the café-adjacent gift shop, all focus turned to the fishing. Dad would remind me again about the storm and the possibility that the fish wouldn't bite.

As soon as our boat left the marina, I felt lost. Everything seemed to look the same, miles and miles of clay cutbanks and rocky bluffs made of shale. I could not comprehend how Dad ever found his way back to where we started. He did, however, have a method. He and Teddy were constantly tossing around names of landmarks like "crow's foot" and "two tits" as if they were Mount Rushmore and the Black Hills.

Crow's foot, as I would learn, was a tree sticking out of the water with dead branches resembling the foot of a crow. Considering I now know one of the best walleye fishing patterns is to seek out the old preflood river channel, my guess is that this bird appendage of a tree used to sit along the old bank and was a landmark for Dad in finding that channel and thus indicative of a good fishing spot.

As for two tits, it was literally a couple of bumps in the terrain up on the shoreline behind the bluffs similar enough to each other and feminine enough in curve and shape to remind him of a couple of perfect breasts. I don't know why that spot was good (for fishing), but I do know we caught fish there.

At one of these spots, I couldn't tell you which, Dad confidently killed the motor and went to work with our gear. He prepared lines with live bait and a rotating spinner in front of it attached by five feet of line to a piece of wire with a weight he called a bottom bouncer. This contraption would keep our bait (night crawler or minnow) near the bottom as the boat slowly trolled or drifted forward and the wire bounced along the underwater terrain.

"Wait 'till I'm ready," he said as he kicked the trolling motor in gear.

"Alright, drop 'er down!"

Teddy struck first about ten minutes later.

"Fish on, Blythe," he said as he leaned back into his chair

with the rod tip high above his head, bobbing forward toward the water as the fish swam against him. When he was exerting effort, you could always hear him breathing heavily through his mouth muffler. He reeled it up near the side of the boat, and Dad stabbed it with the landing net.

As Teddy worked to unhook the fish and put it in our livewell, Dad grabbed something out of a storage compartment that looked like a yellow plastic dumbbell with rope wrapped around the middle. As our boat continued crawling forward, Dad chucked the dumbbell back behind the boat approximately where Teddy had caught his fish. Immediately the dumbbell began rotating as rope peeled off vertically underneath.

"What's that?" I asked.

"It's called a marker buoy. That way we know where we caught the fish and we can troll back past there again later."

Smart.

Now I was waiting for my turn. In order to prepare me, I remember Dad tugging on my line to simulate a hungry walleye nipping, gulping, and then swimming away with my bait. He started with a few short tugs, which would represent the fish tasting or grabbing the bait, and then bigger thumps as he pulled the line down, meaning the fish had the bait in its mouth and was swimming away in the other direction. Still, every single time my line dragged over a rock or through mud or brushed against the least bit of underwater cabbage, I either thought to myself or asked aloud, "Is that a bite?"

A few minutes later, as we circled back past the marker Dad had tossed out, it happened. As hard as one tries to prepare, you almost have to get your first bite before you know what you're feeling for. And from that point on, it becomes an addiction. It didn't feel exactly the way Dad imitated it with his fingers pulling my line, but it was similar enough to bridge the gap. I successfully handled the fish, and soon Dad netted that one as well. It wasn't huge, probably seventeen inches, quite similar to Teddy's first one.

"Nice job, Brett!" Dad said. "There's your first walleye! That's a good eater."

We were just settling in now, I figured, waiting for the monster 'eye! Or the big pike that Dad had told me lived there. This was only the beginning!

We used to have library day once a week back in grade school, basically a forty-five-minute time slot to freely browse and read whatever we could find. A few of us often raced—without running, of course!—to the nonfiction section to grab the most recent edition of the *Guinness Book of World Records*. Thankfully, they put out a new one every year, so if you weren't the fastest speed walker in your grade and someone else got the most recent copy, one of the previous years would do. World records are hard to break, so it would still give you a solid idea of what you were up against if you hoped to get an entry with your name on it.

I would browse through the usual records—world's tallest man, Robert Wadlow at 8'11". That one was probably out of my control genetically. World's longest fingernails might be attainable, but it sounds like a pain in the ass. Plus, the way those things curled around and got all thick and brittle, it seemed pretty disgusting.

The world's largest walleye was twenty-two pounds and eleven ounces, caught out of Greers Ferry Lake in Arkansas by Al Nelson in the spring of '82. Fish records were normally counted by weight, so most lengths were only approximated, but this record was said to be around thirty-six inches.

A walleye over thirty inches is considered by most to be a "fish of a lifetime." The twenty-eight-inch mark is usually the bottom cutoff for a trophy fish, one that might spend its afterlife on a wall above a fireplace, and some states even have "master angler" programs that provide certificates as souvenirs. I would consider any walleye in the mid-twenties to be "big." Walleyes in the range of fourteen to twenty inches are pretty typical for table fare. Anything smaller is usually considered a "tiny" fish, and many bodies of water have a minimum size restriction of fourteen or fifteen inches.

We didn't catch any world records. Or even any fish to last a lifetime. Though we did catch a ton of eaters up to probably nineteen or twenty inches. Though I had caught a bunch of walleyes for the first time in my life, I somehow left the water disappointed.

I'm not sure if any experience could ever have lived up to my lofty expectations. The stories I always heard from my dad and my visual account of Mom's eight-pound hog they brought home on ice—fully intact, just so they could show us—set a pretty high bar in my little brain. I was definitely excited to catch my first Missouri River walleye, and I was excited for all of the rest of them too, but by the end I was left wondering, "Where are all the big ones?"

In my head I had built up the Missouri River as a trophy fish paradise, but I hadn't fully grasped the concept of the different reservoirs yet. Dad would later explain to me that he also fished Lake Oahe, the next reservoir up, near Pierre, South Dakota, which had bigger water and bigger fish. That's where Mom got her big fish too, just months, I believe, before the divorce. I was certainly happy to be on the fishing trip that I was, but, to be honest, I almost felt as though he had pulled a bait-and-switch on me. "Why were we not fishing at Lake Oahe?" I asked. The answer sounded a lot like "Bigger water, longer drive, rougher waves, blah blah blah," but I didn't see what the problem was.

Nevertheless, this trip lit a fire of walleye obsession inside me. It completely changed my perspective on what fishing was and could be compared to the old tossing of a bobber into a small pond or our small, hometown river, which before this trip was the extent of my fishing experience.

Walleye fishing was a totally different ballgame, and even the small ones were bigger than fish I had caught before. Walleye didn't spin in circles like a rambunctious bluegill or flutter upward and look to leap out of the water like a bass; they were more vertically oriented. When they sensed trouble, they went down. Perhaps they also knew not to walk toward the light when their life was threatened. There seemed to be a different integrity to walleye fishing, a certain gravitas that drew me in. I wanted more of it, a lot more. Waiting another year to fish up on Lake Oahe seemed like an eternity.

FISHER (OF) MEN

My Bloemendaal ancestry is full of oversized hands and big old heads. Rarely do I find a person's hands to be their most memorable aspect, even if, for whatever reason, such memories are limited to physical anatomy. Still, most of my friends' first impressions of my dad wind up centering around the handshake experience with "those giant bear paws." My grandpa's hands were even bigger than my dad's, and legend has it that *his* dad's hands were bigger yet.

My last memory of my great grandpa was of him in the care center playing his harmonica, and from my angle it looked like he was just blowing into a couple of baseball mitts, so I'd say the legend checks out. A perfect caricature of my dad alongside his father and grandfather would look like a trio of bobblehead dolls with Hulk fists holding hammers, shovels, and fishing poles.

We're like a bunch of Neanderthals. I say this in the spirit of humor but with a small slice of truth. According to my 23andMe test, I have about double the Neanderthal DNA of the average human being; my previous generations may have had more. The hands and heads continue to thin out down the generations, but it still shows. We big old Dutch boys were built to work. Most everyone up until my generation worked on a farm, lifted heavy things, and understood the working parts of a gas engine.

I only have but the one harmonica memory of my great grandpa, and I don't even remember my great grandma, but I have plenty of imprints from the next generation down. We spent a substantial amount of time with Grandpa and Grandma as a family given that their home in Luverne, Minnesota, was only a short seventeen miles north of our place in Rock Rapids, Iowa. Occasionally us kids, just my brother Brandon and I at that time back then, would get exclusive grandparent time, typically when Dad left town.

I don't remember the reason behind every kid visit with Grandpa and Grandma, but a few of them occurred when Dad left to fish the Missouri River on the adults-only trips. These were bittersweet visits for me, however, as I also knew Luverne was where Dad got on the interstate to continue west toward "The River," as he fondly referred to it. I was always disappointed watching the back end of his outboard motor follow the truck into the distance, aching to ride along on the adventure. I usually got over it after an hour or so, however, especially the time Grandpa let us shoot his BB gun in the basement.

My kid brain was soaking in a cocktail one part confusion and two parts elation over the idea of shooting a gun indoors. It seemed like something that could only be accomplished through sneaky mischief, yet it was sanctioned by Grandpa himself, even initiated by him. Perhaps that was the psychological mind trick to get our minds off Dad leaving. He printed up paper targets of cartoon characters as silly as his own sense of humor, showed us how to work the gun, then sat back in a lawn chair watching, directing, and laughing.

"Get that one with the top hat right in the nose," he'd say.

I'd line up my shot just like I learned from one of Grandpa's seventy plus John Wayne movies and slowly squeeze the trigger. Pop! Rarely were we ever as precise as his call, but we peppered those targets with plenty of little puncture wounds.

"That was close, Brett! Give 'er to Brandon and let him try."

We were so jazzed up about this, we had to show Dad when he returned to pick us up two or three days later. The targets were hung in front of old, worn-out blankets and sheets we used as a backstop. Nevertheless, Brandon missed so wildly on one of his shots that the tiny metal projectile ricocheted off the cement basement wall right into Dad's forehead. I think I recall Grandpa laughing, but I'm pretty sure Dad didn't. The rest of the memory is fuzzy, but I vaguely remember Dad having one of those sidebar adult conversations with Grandpa, the kind that gives kids the sense rules are being made or changed beyond their control.

While our membership to the basement shooting range was short-lived, our local fishing privileges were never revoked. If Dad was going on an epic fish hunt without us, Grandpa was at least willing to take us out for bluegills and sunnies at the ponds on the edge of town. Near as I can tell, Grandpa was every bit as invested as we were in the fish-catching efforts too.

He fished in his Sunday clothes, a button-down shirt and a pair of "slacks" as he called them. Come to think of it, he did most everything dressed this way. I don't think he even owned a pair of jeans. It was his "outfit," another term he used often to refer to almost anything whether it be a set of clothing or a new toy we brought along.

"That's a pretty neat little outfit you got there, Brett."

"It's a toy, Grandpa."

"Oooohhhhhh."

His fishing style was unique unto himself. He was relaxed but observant. Then, when his bobber started to twitch or he felt a bite, he sat at attention on the edge of his lawn chair like a dog who just smelled a rabbit. He had a lean, slow and quiet as if sneaking up on a fly with a swatter. Just when the time was right, thwack! Sometimes his hands were too big and strong for his own good, especially when messing with six-inch bluegill. I imagine there were a handful of them swimming around missing an upper lip after our day at the pond.

He caught plenty too, as did we. Once in a while we would be surprised by a largemouth bass, hollering as if we'd just won the lottery. My brother once caught a tiny muskie of about thirteen inches, one I assumed must have been stocked by the Minnesota DNR. Last time I brought it up, he seemed to think I actually caught it, but I'm pretty sure it was he. One of us sure did, anyway. That's not the sort of thing a young fisherman forgets, as it looks nothing like a bluegill—much longer, toothier, and with shiny vertical stripes down its long, slender, snaky frame.

Grandma even caught a few. I remember Grandpa constantly shouting at her, "Barb, your bobber is down! You have to reel it in now!" I wondered why he sounded so bossy. Something seemed off to me; she couldn't seem to remember what to do the second time. Or the third. Or the tenth. I was none the wiser, but her mind was suffering from the symptoms of Alzheimer's disease. It's an awful beast I wouldn't wish upon anyone, especially when it strikes at such an early age. Matter of fact, it took her away from us in her early 60s.

I never felt safer than when I was sitting on Grandma's lap. She was the kindest, gentlest soul I'd ever known. She would sit there crocheting and humming church hymns more soothing than a pacifier dipped in cough syrup. Sometimes she would pause her work to softly rub my neck and back with her fingernails while continuing to sing. If I were a cat, I would've purred. Good thing I wasn't—I'm allergic.

The sad irony is that as her condition worsened, she lived most of her final days terrified. She didn't know what was happening or who we were, shouting uncharacteristic obscenities at us to get us to leave the room before Dad would take us for a walk through the halls of the care center and explain to us why Grandma yelled so much then. Prior to the disease, I never heard her shout or use any word even as inflammatory as "darn."

If I could rid the planet of any two things, it would be Alzheimer's and mosquitos. In that order.

I know she was with us when we fished, sitting next to Grandpa in her own chair with her own rod and reel, but her character is fuzzy in my mind, probably because it was fuzzy in hers. What I can tell you, though, is based on stories and assurances from my dad and my grandfather—she both loved to catch and to eat fish. And, as Dad would let us know many years later at his second parental funeral, she loved dancing with Grandpa.

As her condition worsened, Grandpa had to take on an even greater role as caretaker. Fortunately, he was extremely well-suited for the job. He was an excellent family man, but beyond that he was also a minister at his local community church. He gave much-heralded sermons from behind the pulpit, and he was wonderful with the community relations. Everyone in town knew who he was, and everyone had wonderful things to say about him. He earned the title "Reverend."

He did hospital visits. He did house visits. He prayed for people. He counseled people. He was a large physical figure with a heart of gold, and he was everyone's rock to stand on, shoulder to cry on, and set of arms to lift you up when you were down.

Strangely enough, I went a lot of years of my life having never heard one of Grandpa's sermons in person. For one thing, he did live in a different town and was part of a different church. For another, we were not the regular churchgoers one might have expected as grandchildren of a minister. I always wondered if that upset or disappointed him. If it did, he certainly never let it show to us.

One Sunday Dad decided we would attend Grandpa's service. It was surreal how some of the members immediately knew we were his grandchildren, probably because they knew Dad, who was ushering us to our seats, but it seemed like kid magic to me at the time. They began inundating us with compliments about what an amazing man Grandpa was and what he had done for them personally and spiritually. The buzz was contagious, and I became even more excited to hear him speak in his element. This wasn't just Grandpa anymore, this was "Pastor B.," evidently a huge public figure in the town of Luverne, Minnesota, as I was learning.

I have always struggled with the concept of faith, to believe in something you can't physically see or understand. I learned much about Grandpa's faith that day, though. He spoke with firm conviction yet zero condescension. His goal was not to scare or manipulate anyone into believing anything, he simply lived the example and put it out there for anyone to take it or leave it.

I don't know if that sermon, or any other for that matter, made me believe in faith or God, but I do know it 100% made me believe in Grandpa.

Certainly, there were days as a young child I sort of accepted Christianity at face value. It was pretty much pervasive in my community in northwest Iowa, and until taking history and religion classes in high school and college, I always assumed Christianity *was* religion. I didn't know there were a host of other religions with different beliefs, different gods, different everything. The plan seemed pretty straightforward back then: if you're good and you believe, you go to heaven, and if you're bad and don't believe, you get a fiery alternative.

Years later, Grandpa succumbed to a similar neurodegenerative condition. I did get the chance, though, to ask him about his faith a couple years before he lost the capacity to explain it. His answer then was a little surprising, but looking back on it now with even more comprehension of life's grayer hues, not so much so.

"Brett," he said to me, "I'm honestly not completely sure if God exists, but the way I see it is that I'd rather be on his side if he does."

Somehow it was comforting to hear a man of unwavering faith be humble enough to admit he may be wrong. I also don't know if Heaven exists, but if it does, I think there is a chance Grandpa and Grandma are sitting side-by-side in their lawn chairs waiting for the fish to bite. And, if my dad is right, they'll go out dancing afterward.

As for me, I'd have to keep fishing for answers.

Me with Granpda and
Grandma on that lap of safety.

THE BIG BIG WATER

IT WAS MUCH TOO EARLY for humans to be walking around, but Dad's emerald metallic-green Chevy Blazer and blue Lund Cherokee fishing boat were both fully packed, and we had five hours of road time before we could fish. Still groggy, and probably cranky, I slumped down into the backseat to doze off for another couple hours.

About a hundred miles west of home, I came alive (for good this time), gobbled down my cinnamon roll, and slurped up my orange juice. My excitement was building, and we couldn't get there fast enough. It's Lake "Freaking" Oahe, baby! The big water! No, the *big* big water. Most importantly, it was Dad's favorite place to fish.

Chamberlain and Lake Francis Case are on the way to Pierre for a northwest Iowa traveler, so we got to see the single-adjective big water along the way, which I thought was neat symbolism for my own stepladder journey to fishing big water. The view got my blood pumping and served as both a fond reminder of the previous year and a teaser for what was to come.

The visual climax for me was finally arriving at the land bridge of Lake Oahe, a spectacle of a dirt wall standing firm in the face of 370,000 acres of flowing water. Dad also built the suspense for us during our five-hour drive.

"You're not gonna believe your eyes when you see how big that water is! And we're gonna drive right over it! It's takes a full two minutes to get across."

Dad has a way of making almost anything seem epic, but in this instance, he didn't have to try very hard. It's amazing to think humans were able to engineer something so massive. As you approach, you see the river in the spillway underneath, which is more than two hundred feet below where you are about to drive.

Slowly you roll up on top, and the reservoir dazzles your eyes with its sheer volume as well as the magnificent cliff-like bluffs that shape the shoreline, cutting in and out of the water like mountains in a Bob Ross painting. Time stopped long enough for me to take a series of mental pictures until we crossed the two miles of water. Having finally seen its glory, the anticipation was almost too much, but we still had a long, curvy, hilly drive to the boat ramp from which we were launching. Good things are worth waiting for, but waiting was oh so hard having already seen the water!

Once we arrived at the ramp, Dad still had to prepare the boat for launch. The tarp had to snap off, the plug had to go in lest we sink, the motor had to be trimmed to avoid scraping on pavement, and gear needed to be transported from our land vehicle to our water vessel. I even helped occasionally when Dad would shout to pull my attention back from the water.

After what seemed like an eternity, a feeling I'm sure is partly my fault because I likely did little to nothing to help the launching process (what kid could focus on mundane minutiae at a time such as this?!), we were in the boat and on the water. I simply couldn't grasp how big everything was. So much water. So many bluffs. So much taller and much more imposing than the ones I remember from Lake Francis Case.

At one point, running on plane through the middle of the lake, my dad pointed at the depth finder reading over two hundred feet! Even our boat ride to our first fishing spot was longer, in the neighborhood of fifteen miles to the mouth where the Cheyenne River empties into Lake Oahe. Finally, after getting up in the dark, driving five hours, getting food and our fishing licenses, driving to the boat ramp, launching the boat, and driving to our spot, we were ready to drop some lines in the water.

Dad always occupied the bow as he ran the trolling motor to chase down and keep us on top of the roaming walleyes of the reservoir. These days Bluetooth remotes offer the captain much more freedom, but at that place in time, bow-mounted trolling motors were run locally with tiller handles or wired foot pedals. Each time we made a trip like this, it took me a while to get into the groove of feeling the bottom, noticing bites, and knowing when to set the hook. A lot of times I would crank my head in Dad's direction and watch him work his magic looking to steal a pointer or two.

It always got intense for me when Dad would start to get a bite. You would know because he'd lean into it and start reaching his rod tip to feed the bait back to the fish, like Van Damme setting up his enemy. I would be on the edge of my seat waiting for him to pull the trigger. And then, like Steven Seagal snapping a thug's arm in a clean break, he would crack the rod as it bent over and shook, the fishy perpetrator violently trying to free itself.

I learned a lot about how to play a fish by watching my dad. He was in no hurry to reel in anything. As long as he maintained the proper line tension, and the fish was still pulling, he patiently waited and only picked up slack when the fish gave it, always balancing pressure. It was a microcosm of how he played life, patient yet aggressive. He taught best by example, and I was always watching.

My not-yet stepmom, Trish, was along with us. She was a sun tanner first, and an extreme one at that. She didn't use the sissy sunblock reserved for our tender skin, she brought out the tanning oils after cleansing her hands of that Coppertone crap. She ran cold and loved the heat, preferring to be well done, crispy like fried chicken. Perhaps Dad liked it that way too. I'm not sure.

I had a tough time accepting the idea of having a stepmother. To be fair, change in general was difficult for me and still is. I remember feeling Trish was moving too fast to fill a spot in the household that I wasn't convinced was open yet. Regardless of how measured she would have been in her approach, though, it wouldn't have mattered because I still thought Mom and Dad would be together again someday. I missed my mom, and I had wished she was the one putting on my sunblock. I was adjusting, but occasional triggers would pull me out of the moment before the fish pulled me back in.

That particular trip, I believe, was our last weekend before school started, toward the end of August. It was hotter than devil's spit, as can often be the case on Lake Oahe in the peak of summer. For all intents and purposes, the lake was nestled into the Badlands of South Dakota, after all. Each day approached or topped one hundred degrees, and we had to find the fish deep at a depth of thirty to forty feet.

One might think that a kid of my age would be more interested in swimming in such conditions. I would've scoffed at such a suggestion. You don't swim on a fishing trip. Get that weak child's play out of my face! I was thirteen going on thirty and looking for trophy walleyes.

This particular day of note was also fairly calm, which can make things even tougher. For a while, Dad struggled to get us on fish, but then we found a really nice pod on a prominent main lake point. Each pass we would pick up a fish or two, and nice ones at that; I'm thinking they were in the 19-to-23-inch range. I remember they had "cheekability." As walleyes mature and fill out, their cheeks get thick and pouty, giving you a couple of extra bonus cuts. Cheek meat is different than the rest of the fish, slightly chewy and a little richer. They are sometimes referred to as "freshwater scallops," a true delicacy.

Eventually Trish hooked into another fish, and you could tell by the look on her face and the bend of the rod that this fish was even bigger. It was dogging her hard and taxing the strength of that monofilament line and graphite Berkley Lightning Rod. As it finally neared the surface, the water was clear enough without the chop we could see most of the action. The fish continued making violent efforts to escape, diving and thrashing about in the first few feet of the water column. Eventually that finny bastard was outmatched as Dad snared it with the landing net.

The fish was in the mid-to-upper twenty-inch range, and Dad estimated it to be around six pounds. It was certainly her personal best. It was one of those moments that could make an early teenage fishing junkie both excited and jealous all at once. Of course she would catch the biggest fish. Maybe I wanted it too much. Maybe I too needed to spend half of the day suntanning with my rod unattended. Yes, sadly, it could make me a little bitter. I bit my lip and pushed myself through the moment much the way I used to do when I was forced to smile for family pictures. "Nice fish, Trish."

Either the feeding frenzy had just ended or Trish's monster had stirred up too much chaos on a calm day and spooked the rest out of there. We never got another bite, and eventually we left to clean our catch for the day, cheek meat and all. Dad made us kings of the cleaning station yet again.

Watching other members of our boat catch fish would be cool for a while, but I was still of the self-centered age when not catching them myself could leave me frustrated and disinterested, especially if others were getting the big ones. I would start desperately looking for answers as to why I was not catching fish when other people were. Did I have enough line out? Too much?

Had I missed my bait being stolen, and should I check it? Should I change my spinner blade, a new size, a new color?

Eventually all of those questions would be answered once I reeled in a nice fish, at which point I would be quick to tell everyone else what I was using and what I did. Confidence in fishing cycles through extreme highs and lows. One moment you feel like you don't know what the hell you're doing, and the next it's your duty to tell the world how to get it done.

Once I would find a groove, my engagement would reach levels of obsession. Through heightened senses, I could feel everything under the water via spurts of hyper awareness in the midst of peak opportunity. I wasn't going to miss even the smallest bite, and I was going to actively play my line almost as if I could will any fish watching to suck it in. Sometimes I would notice the rest of the boat was quiet too, everyone standing up and holding their rods. We were all in the same zone. Fishing nirvana.

A day after Trish's hog came in the boat, I was in one of these grooves and waiting intensely for my next bite. Soon something impeded the movement of my line. I patiently waited to see if the impedance would continue or if it was simply a rock or a tree about to let go as our boat trolled us forward. A second tug, then a third, and I anxiously reached my rod tip back, just as I had watched my father do, to feed line to what I hoped was a fish. And when I could tell it made its last gulp, got heavy with weight and started to pull, wham! I set that hook as hard as I could and barely budged that fish!

Only a few seconds into the fight, I could tell it was significantly bigger than any I had on before. It was heavy to the point of straining my wrists and forearms. When it made its first run, I feared I was about to lose the rod out of my hand, so I stuck the bottom end into the side of my belly to use it as a lever. Dad, of course, was coaching me through it.

"Let her run if she runs. You pull too hard, she'll snap your line."

"I know! I'm trying!"

"Now pull up some line."

"Okay, I am. Is this a big one?"

"It's looking pretty big, yeah. Just take your time."

"It's almost here! I can't see it yet. I don't want it to break my line."

I then felt a hard thump thump thump. And then weightlessness.

Somehow the fish managed to shake itself free, and I reeled up an empty hook. Perhaps I wasn't able to get the hooks deep enough into the fish's skin with my little Tweety Bird arms. Or maybe that wily old walleye simply outplayed me. Or maybe a person just has to experience loss and a near miss before they're ready to welcome success.

I felt like my dog had just died. Or somebody had canceled Christmas. I had my first really big fish, so close to the boat, and then in an instant it was all taken away from me. Or I managed to lose it. It's all in how you frame it, I suppose. The latter can be a true confidence killer, and after another near miss later in the day, the wind was pretty well knocked out of my sails.

I had a hard time thinking of it this way at the time, but the ones that get away can sometimes keep you coming back just as motivated as the big ones you catch. It leaves a bit of unfinished business to tend to in the future. Still, it is a little unfortunate my most vivid memories of such a magical place come down to the fish I didn't get in the boat. The rest of the scenes blend into misty generalities.

I remember the fish biting harder than I had ever experienced before. I remember them being harder to reel in. I remember my wrist hurting at the end of the day. I remember there being bigger lulls in the day, perhaps catching fewer fish than at Chamberlain but most definitely bigger fish. I remember how they would dive straight down boatside as we attempted to net them. And I remember Dad ramping up anticipation with his words: "They get bigger."

For me, Lake Oahe is a feeling. It's fishing, serious fishing. It's summertime heat (because we could only go after the school year let out). It's big walleyes. It's your crappiest, dirtiest shirt that you don't care about getting dirtier. When it gets flat calm out, it's the bugs. Then it's the catfish. Then it's Dad cannonballing into the water when you're half asleep and scaring the living crap out of you. Or bursting into an Aerosmith chorus with "DUDE looks like a lay-day!" and having the same shocking effect.

It's the drive out there, the hills, the early glimpses of the water. It's Van Halen, more specifically Van Haggar, blasting on the CD player of Dad's Blazer. In fact, I now remember Dad lip-synching "I Can't Stop Loving You" to Trish while Brandon and I were riding in the backseat, which prompted Brandon to ask two or three times over, "Are you guys getting married?!" They weren't, at least not yet. I'm not sure why I don't remember much of Brandon fishing during these trips, but I certainly remember that car ride now. Was I so zoned in on fish that I hadn't noticed my own little brother?

It's bigger waves, constantly watching the wind, and Dad telling you "We wouldn't want to be out on the other side of the lake right now." It's always looking for a bigger walleye. It's Dad saying "Oooh, I just marked a pig of a fish down there! Somebody catch it!" It's big points, it's deep water, and it's bottom bouncers and night crawlers until it becomes trolling crankbaits. And, eventually, it's Dad holding up a six-pound fish to the heavens and proclaiming, "Now THAT is a Pierre walleye!"

It's going over the day's results, studying maps at night, rechecking the weather, and making a plan for tomorrow. It's picking the right boat ramp. It's making long boat runs if the fishing is slow where you are. It's names of spots—Sunset, Cheyenne, Pike Haven, Peoria Flats. It's finding a great spot on a spot, usually a nice long point sticking out into the water, and slowly working it back and forth until we get 'em. It's deciding when to move, when to go deeper, when to go shallower. Faster or slower? What color spinner blade? Half or full crawler? Switch to crankbaits this afternoon?

It's a small slice of Missouri River walleye fishing flowing in my blood just as it did with my dad, the action hero of my childhood. I thought we'd be fishing Lake Oahe forever.

RIVER RATS

Life as a kid in small-town Iowa was pretty free and easy, especially during the summer break from school. We didn't spend a lot of time in the house. There were a lot of football games in the backyard and at the park, pick-up basketball games as well. Once bicycles entered the equation, our world grew exponentially. We were allowed to go almost anywhere as long as it was within city limits and we were back home by the "six o'clock whistle."

I don't know if this was a norm in other towns, but Rock Rapids had an emergency alert siren put in place to warn its residents of oncoming tornadoes or other strong storms. Every day, however, at noon and six o'clock, they "blew the whistle" to indicate what we called dinner and supper (or lunch and dinner, depending on one's terminology). If you heard the whistle at any other time of day, it was wise to take cover. To this day, I am regimented about mealtime, and I can either blame or thank that whistle.

During those hours of freedom, our bikes most often took us down to the Rock River. Mastering the art of riding a bike while carrying a fishing rod and tackle box takes a little bit of time, but we quickly became experts. The rod simply became an extension of the handlebars. The handle of the tacklebox was secured by a pinky finger on either side. The contents of the tackle boxes were relatively light for ease of travel—a variety of weights, split shots and bullet sinkers, and a few hooks, maybe a bobber or two.

We'd grab some night crawlers at the local bait shop (a dude's garage with a sign, really) and maybe a can of corn from the cupboard or some chicken liver if we were fortunate enough to get ahold of it. If we found a crawdad by the river near our fishing spot, the crawly critter would wind up on somebody's line too.

I always thought the can of corn was an interesting bait choice, but Dad actually taught us that one. For one reason or another, the carp in the river seemed to love corn for dinner. And since our nightly meals with Dad often consisted of a daily rotation of canned corn or canned green beans with meatloaf or roast and mashed potatoes on the side—at least on the days we didn't order takeout—we had a healthy inventory and were willing to share some with the fish.

The trick to river fishing is finding the right spot near the current but not so directly in the current that your line washes away before fish can grab it. Little eddies and slack-water locations were key, maybe a bend in the river or a point sticking out into the flowing water, or perhaps some fallen tree branches slowing the water's pace. Ripples on the surface could indicate rocks underneath, a classic hiding spot for river fish if you could present a bait without getting stuck.

The target was anything with fins and gills. At the Rock River this was most often catfish, bullheads, carp, and suckers. Carp are widely considered garbage fish in America, but they were one of my favorites back then because they were easy to catch, grew long and chubby, and always put up a good fight. It seems you can always count on a few carp to hold your attention at the Rock River.

I was told there were some walleye swimming there as well,

and I had heard of some being caught, but I was never fortunate enough to catch one myself. I did occasionally see someone catch a northern pike, and as a result, I started bringing long, skinny crankbaits—essentially fake fish made of wood or plastic with a bill in the front that makes them dive and wobble through the water—hoping to entice one of those, but I never did. The only thing I can remember catching on a crankbait down there were mooneyes. Ugly suckers those things were, with gargantuan eyes taking up way too much of their facial real estate, an underbite jaw with sharp teeth, and a sickly iridescent glow to their scales. If they were any bigger, they would be a bona fide sea monster. And they bled like mad, all over your hands and the jeans your mom told you not to get dirty. Cursed fish.

Fishing down at the river was as much about the adventure as anything else. We spent hours traversing sandbars and steep shorelines, walking across the various little dams, perhaps planning out architectural blueprints for some kind of fort or treehouse, a little hideout that could be ours someday by the river. And I can't forget the most important task, finding the perfect stick for a rod holder.

Ideally it would be shaped like a perfect slingshot, one main branch and two offshoots above for a groove to hold a fishing rod. If you got three branches which were able to hold two rods, that was a bonus. You want it tall enough to stick into the ground and elevate the rod a little but not too tall lest it become unwieldy. It also needed the right thickness, perhaps the diameter of a nickel, just strong enough to hold the rod against the current or a fish.

Trips usually involved a couple of my close friends in the neighborhood and eventually my brother when he got old enough. My most frequent fishing companion to the river was my friend Andy, who lived across the alley from my house. He was a scrawny, crewcut kid who loved baseball and his bike. He was a character from *The Sandlot* if ever I knew one. He was also quite shy; I was as well, but he was the only friend I ever had who made me feel outgoing.

He was also the most fishing-oriented of all my friends. Some may have been into it for an hour or so, but their interest would fade well before mine. Others didn't really know how to cast or how to tie a line, so I spent more time helping them than fishing myself. But Andy was a fishing partner, not a tagalong. We could both have lasted until the sun went down if our parents had let us. Besides, we had always heard the fishing gets best right at sundown. This is the only way I know how to fish, believing the best action is only minutes away.

Brandon and I also dubbed him "B-Button Andy" because of his unique video game skill. For game noobs, the old classic Nintendo had two main action buttons, A and B. Some games, *Bass Masters Classic*, for example, would require you to push the B button as rapidly as possible to complete a task. In this case, each press of the button was a crank of the reel to pull in a trophy bass.

There is no one else I know who could push a button faster and with more intensity than Andy. It was a spectacle to behold as he cranked up that right shoulder, stuck his tongue out, and went to town, his thumb firing like a piston in a car engine. We would tag-team video games this way, everybody playing their best part. As soon as any task required a rapid button push, we quickly tossed the controller over to B-Button Andy.

Brandon still credits some of our current skills to our days spent video game fishing. You see, you couldn't just push the B button as fast as possible to haul in a fish, you had to play it a little. If the fish started making a hard run and you still pushed the B button as fast as possible, the excess tension would snap the line.

It's all about balance, give and take. Same thing holds true in the real world. You have to maintain a medium level of tension, whether it means reeling up or giving back, until you win the war of attrition. Unless, of course, you're cheating and just using 100-

pound-test braided line which could drag a dead body ashore if need be.

Dad would take us down to the river as well, especially before we earned our biking freedom. One particular night, after many trips of nothing more than carp, catfish, and bullheads, Dad was about to show us something different. While my brother and I were running around trying to find our own best fishing spot, Dad was casting a night crawler right on the edge of a current seam and letting it settle into an eddy at the river bend where I presume there were a few rocks. Minutes later he yelled, "Brando! Come real this in!"

"Brando," one could gather, is my brother's nickname. It's simple, but it rolls off the tongue well. At times we also add "Commando" at the end for a nifty rhyme. His most peculiar nickname, though, he gave to himself at his preschool graduation ceremony. The teacher was going down the line asking each student to say their name into the microphone. When it was his turn, he stuck out his chest.

"BRANDON. JAMES. BLOEMENDAAL!"

For some reason he decided to shout his in staccato form, elevating his voice another notch with each word and punctuating each part as if it were its own sentence. When later prompted to reveal to the audience what he wanted to be when he grew up, he morphed into a karate pose, furrowed his brow, and said with intensity, "A fighter."

After hearing Dad's yell, we sprinted over to his spot on the riverbank. Brando Commando grabbed the rod and fought that fish hard. When the war ended, he pulled in a respectable small-mouth bass that splashed in the mud till Dad grabbed its bottom lip between his thumb and forefinger. I didn't even know those fish were in there! I thought my dad was a genius. We wound up catching two or three more in that same spot thereafter.

At times, soon after my parents divorced, Dad would drive down to the river with us and a bag of takeout food from the local drive-in. He'd park the car at the bank of the river as we sat just watching it flow. We would finish our food and then dig into our hot fudge malts while listening to classic 80s bands like Aerosmith and Heart. I absolutely loved those evenings. Dad would later confess he was just making it up on the fly; he had no clue what the hell to do with us to keep us entertained. Given the circumstances, I was as content as I could be and more than happy with his efforts.

There is something soothing about water. It makes you feel at home. After all, somewhere up the family tree we all have an ancestor who once sported a tail and perhaps dreamt of one day breathing air. Almost everywhere I go in life, if I have free time, I seek out the water. When I had business trips in Chicago, I took walks along the pier at Lake Michigan. When I went to San Francisco, my first stop was always the bay. If at a park in a suburb, I stroll around looking for a pond.

Anytime we were riding in either parent's car and we saw some kind of water, I would always ask, "Are there fish in there?" Oftentimes in the spring after a bunch of rain, farmers' fields would fill up with water in low-lying areas which were dry the week before. Part of me wondered, perhaps hoped, there would be fish in there. If I just cast a line, could I catch something? This was especially true during the floods of 1993, as there were tons of new bodies of water that popped up everywhere. Both parents somehow talked me out of trying.

Those same floods led to a lot of destruction in my hometown. The Rock River spilled over its banks for many weeks on end. Nearly the entire park was destroyed. Animals in the petting zoo either drowned or escaped as their cages were crushed. Some people lost homes. Some people had basements flooded with water. "Sandbagging" became a new buzzword around town. The golf course became a lake.

I knew how bad this event was, but I also couldn't help being fascinated by it. All I could think about was going down to the water to see the whole mess. I don't think Dad ever let us get too close when the water was at its peak, but I remember much of the destruction I saw after the water started to recede by maybe half, the water still raging at an incredible speed.

There were roads and sidewalks which used to wind through the park near the river. Entire chunks of concrete were missing as if the flood waters took a bite out of them like a chocolate chip cookie. Most of the metal fencing was crumpled like cheap paper clips from a discount store. Sand and silt were deposited everywhere, making the shorelines look like sand dunes in a desert.

There was also a concrete bridge spanning the river that had been lifted up, rotated about ninety degrees forward, and dumped about fifty feet from where it used to sit. For a number of years after they rebuilt the bridge, the old chunks still sat there, half of them sticking out of the water, creating a new current break and a popular fishing spot.

I had assumed people moved it—with big cranes or wrecking balls or something, though I didn't have any good ideas as to why —until I was told the water was the culprit. How could water break cement? Kid magic.

As neat as it was to have a river right there in my own town, normally it's not all that big. During the flood, though, it was almost as majestic as the Missouri. At one point in time, the Missouri too was flooded on purpose when they built the dams. Soon enough, however, this water of the Rock River would recede, and things would eventually return to normal.

The floods that year did affect the Missouri River as well. Despite the fact that the dams and reservoirs were built for flood control, there was still only so much they could do with such a ridiculous amount of water in the system. A lot of the bait, the smaller fish like rainbow smelt that fed the bigger walleyes, wound up being lost through the turbines at the various dams, and the fishing got tough for a few years.

Perhaps it's a bit demeaning to refer to smaller fish as simply "bait," since they are their own fish living their own fishy lives, but fisher people tend to categorize them as if they were just food pellets in a fish tank helping to beef up the predatory game fish they're looking to reel in. If you ask someone for a fishing report, the discussion often turns to the quality of the bait in the system. Too much bait makes it difficult to entice a bite, with fish spoiled by choice; not enough causes starving fish to grab anything that moves but look gaunt once you bring them topside. It's very much a Goldilocks sort of thing as you want it just right.

I remember this very well because I was right on the cusp of making my first trip at this point, but Dad didn't want to take us for fear of disappointment of poor fishing. Or perhaps he used it as an excuse to make us wait another couple of years. Nevertheless, instead of making my first trip at ten, we eventually wound up going when I was around age twelve.

We didn't even do a lot of fishing at the Rock River in 1993. For a while the water was obviously too high and moving too quickly to fish. There was too much debris in the water and the clarity was much too turbid. Even once it settled down, I suspect it suffered the same fate as the Missouri with the bait being washed away and fish struggling in the environment. But carp were a hearty species. There were always carp.

The Rock River was never my best fishing, but it was where I developed the love for the sport and the adventure. It was our river, where we explored, found new spots, played with techniques and presentations, and found our own fish. You know that old saying, something about teaching a man to fish? That's where we learned to fish.

BAND GEEK

IT's 3:20 on a weekday as I push through the doors of our high school cafeteria and greet the balmy spring air on my way to golf practice. I make small talk with a friend, classmate, and teammate of mine as we walk our way to the parking lot. After putting my backpack in the car, I start putting on the act.

"Ah crap," I say, "I forgot something in my locker. I'll see you out on the golf course."

Now walking back through those same doors, most of my fellow students are gone. I walk past the cafeteria. My locker is to the right. I take a left, toward the band room.

I am a band geek. More specifically, I am a closet band geek. What I really wanted to play was guitar, but that's not really "a thing" around here. No parent would spend such money for a "toy." It's just a pipe dream, something to watch on TV. So, I settled for sax, but it's a damn good second choice. It's sexy and cool like Kenny G. and Bill Clinton. Even its name sounds like sex.

Plenty of my other friends, and the "cool kids," are in band as well, but they're not *in it* in it. They goof off a lot during practice. They purposefully play wrong things at times just to piss off the director. They talk when they should be playing. And they most certainly do not bring their instruments home to practice outside of school, for such a move would permanently brand you as a geek and ruin your high school career.

Not that being on the golf team makes it, but it doesn't break it so much either. Not being out for track, though, golf's parallel sport on our calendar, is an unforgivable sin in the eyes of the football coaches and some players. I paid a hefty price for that as well in our little *Friday Night Lights* of a northwest Iowa town. I've mostly made peace with that by now; I can't afford more back injuries anyway.

Hurrying down the hallway, my face is a little flushed from the anxiety of possibly being found out. Fortunately, as I enter the room, no one has noticed me yet. I see my saxophone sitting in its assigned place on the shelf along with every other instrument our director had asked each of us to take home and practice. Yes, I tend to do what I am told, but I also take it home for me. I love playing it.

To be safe, I head out the side door and avoid the main entrance to the school as I leave for the second time and head back to my Grand Prix. I put the instrument on the floor of the backseat and drive to the golf course.

Something always seemed off to me about my school and my town growing up. I'm sure every school has some number of bullies picking on kids, but there is another theme I noticed, and I'm not sure it's entirely pervasive elsewhere. There was this attitude across the student body that it's very unbecoming of you to care about something. You could be good at something, but you weren't supposed to *try*, if that makes sense.

Raising your hand in class was a complete faux pas. You were supposed to sit there staring at your desk acting like "this bullshit is stupid" and waiting for a teacher to call on you. Even better, if the teacher did call on you, you ought not to let on that you knew the answer. It was almost as if knowing the square root of 361 would make your dick shrivel up and invert back inside your pelvis. The answer is 19, by the way, and I can still urinate quite normally.

Not even golf practice was a safe haven for someone who cared about things. I had been razzed a handful of times for "posing" too long on my follow-through after my swing. Another incident was over my collared golf shirt. Because it had a collar on it and it was a golf shirt.

"Hey! Look at the PGA pro Bloemendaal there! Gonna be a big tour star someday!"

Apparently, one was supposed to wear either a T-shirt or a hooded sweatshirt. Not that there's anything wrong with that either. It just seemed a little psychotic for the one person wearing a golf shirt at a golf meet to be the outsider and the brunt of verbal assaults from his own teammates.

Looking back, though, I have to admit I didn't own it either. I felt uncomfortable and lacked confidence wearing it, the whole time afraid they were going to think exactly what they wound up saying. I wanted to be on a team that cared about the sport, but I wasn't. It's easier to be cynical than talented, and that's often where our small school landed on things when we weren't competitive. At times I even joined my teammates in calling out other schools for being "too serious." I wanted to be appropriately serious, but I also wanted to fit in with my team. They could probably sense my conflict, and this was their way of pulling me back to their side.

After the meet, the assault got more physical. I entered the school van after dropping my clubs in the back. The aforementioned antagonists were waiting in the back seat. They grabbed me, pulled me down between the seats, held me there, and proceeded to rough up my head and hair, wrench my neck a little, and smack me around a bit. They never meant fatal harm, but they wanted to make me more than a little uncomfortable as they laughed and demeaned my self-esteem.

Again, I don't mean to say bullying isn't commonplace everywhere humans walk, but my teammates' purpose, their "why," seemed different. They appeared to be operating from a headspace to which I couldn't relate. It all seemed so senseless, but maybe I just didn't understand. Or perhaps I'm merely reading too deeply into it, a sin for which I'm often guilty.

As I grew older, it became clear my misstep at the time was failing to realize life was much better lived true to oneself, letting the chips fall where they may. I spent too much time fence-sitting for my own ass's good, stepping toward who I was but lacking enough confidence to act decisively and therefore leaving myself vulnerable to those looking for an easy target. We all had a lot to learn, whether we wanted to or not. Fitting in isn't easy, and perhaps it's not even desirable.

WHO DO YOU WANT TO BE FOREVER?

I WOULD GUESS ONLY a few can claim to have a true and obvious calling in life. Perhaps God spoke to them in a dream, or in a Chili's after having a few too many margaritas. Or maybe the ghost of Jimi Hendrix floated down and landed on the headstock of their Fender and said, "Dude! Even I wasn't this good at your age!" Or some dead baseball player walked out of their cornfield and told them to "build it" and "they will come."

What about the rest of us, though? Do we trust our high school counselors? Do we just do whatever our mom or dad did? Try to take thirty-eight different online "which-career-fits-you" quizzes? Throw darts at a list drawn on a crumpled piece of notebook paper taped to our bedroom wall? Save up some money and go ask a fortune teller? Go after our favorite reality-TV-show jobs like *Deadliest Catch* or *American Chopper*? Pick something related to our favorite class in high school? Pick something that might suck but also pays a lot of money?

I don't know how someone is supposed to pick the thing they want to do for the rest of their life at age eighteen, but I can tell you how I did it. It's pretty sexy and mind blowing, so prepare yourself.

During my last year of high school, I remember thinking how

intimidating finance was and how much of life revolved around money. I was nervous about having to deal with all those adult finance things when I graduated. I was worried that lenders would take advantage of me for not understanding credit scores and interest rates or that misplacing a decimal or comma would cost me an extra million dollars on a used car purchase. Small mistakes seemed to have such large, irreversible consequences to me, like I was writing my life with a pen rather than a pencil and Wite-Out hadn't been invented yet. Navigating this gauntlet of adult-speak jargon terrified me. So, I thought to myself, "What if I just major in it? Then I would be pretty good at it, and it would be less scary."

Brett, you radical risk-taker, you! Way to shoot for the stars! Aim high you sultan of sensibility! Think big you prince of practicality! Follow your passions you prolific pragmatist!

Perhaps I am being too hard on myself. A major and/or career choice absolutely does not have to be super sexy. And not everyone is going to get their dream job right out of the gate. Also don't misconstrue this as me having anything against a career in finance. It can be a wonderful field for a lot of people. In my case, though, instead of following a dream or a passion, I went about as far to the other end of the spectrum as possible. Not only was it a safe choice, but I basically picked something I didn't like. And was afraid of. On purpose, nonetheless.

I mean, I could have just taken a few courses to get more comfortable over time. Maybe, *maybe* gotten a minor in finance. Instead, I was trying to build my whole career around it. It really makes me question why we put eighteen-year-olds into such a consequential decision tree when most of them know almost nothing about what they want. Granted, we can always change course later, but between the money investment and the time commitment, so many of us feel obligated to forge on, especially if we make it through the first year or two.

So, I majored in finance. And then I made a subtle shift to economics. Later, realizing the amount of overlap, I decided to major in both. A double major in finance and banking (my alma mater's title of one major) and economics (just one word). And a minor in accounting. I hate accounting. Good god, what was I doing to myself!

At any rate, I made it through college rather successfully. I even enjoyed many, though not all, of my classes. There were a couple of reasons for this, and they both had to do with my type-A, achievement-oriented personality. Success was just getting an "A." Of course, I hated some of the classes. Learning wasn't supposed to be fun, and neither would work be later in life as I was told by most authority figures. Speaking of which, reason number two: my overzealous desire to appease authority. You can call me a teacher's pet if you want, but the point is I got a lot of satisfaction from excelling at something difficult and pleasing people I looked up to.

To be clear, I thoroughly enjoyed college and most of the material, primarily because I loved the theory, the academia, and the creative aspect of it. The real-world applications never lived up to the world spinning around in my head or the one I inferred from the tutelage of my amazing professors. I also loved the college lifestyle, immersing myself in the campus experience and thriving in the independent structure and pacing of the environment.

Being only four years and divided into semesters, college always seemed like a series of sprints I could run at my own pace and in a style most suitable to me. I could lay it all out on the line and be done with it. Then there was room to take a break and reflect on what I'd learned and how I'd grown and to prepare for the next level after some well-earned celebration.

But if college is a sprint, a career is a marathon, maybe a double marathon. Actually, it's more a constant run consuming the rest of one's life until retirement. I think work can be set up to have more intermediate goals, and perhaps some organizations do this well, but it just seems to me the corporate world is a lot more like the movie *Groundhog Day*. Moreover, instead of having a new professor to impress every semester, you might have mostly the same boss and management for years or decades. Some of the day-to-day work might stay the same. Even projects can draw out for years without very many milestones in the middle.

After a number of years, it occurred to me I was sprinting a marathon and flat out fucking exhausted. Oh yeah, and I didn't even like running! I was okay at running, but I had to practice and exercise a lot harder than other runners. First into the gym (office) in the morning and last to leave in the evening. That's how you prove yourself, right?

What was I trying to prove and to whom? To my corporate colleagues that I could be great at something I didn't enjoy? To myself that I could hang with the big boys in the investment world? Proving to myself I actually liked the contents of my working day, not just the fulfillment and reward of completing something difficult?

Has there ever been something in your life you were good at but just hated doing? Perhaps it was a class in school? Maybe you got good marks, but it was just so stressful, draining, and unful-filling to do?

For example, I have always been good at math, but I hated doing it, especially under time pressure and even more so with consequences of performance. We're digging further down the rabbit hole here and further back along my timeline. Having to do flashcards in grade school and competing against other class-mates was a freaking nightmare. I'm pretty sure the first time I sweat in my life, like a real puberty-style sweat, was during one of these flash card competitions. I could feel the warmth come over my face and my palms start to clench and clam up as the rotation approached my desk.

The funny thing is, outside of a couple uber geniuses in my class, I usually beat almost everyone else. I always got A's for grades in math classes. But it made me so uncomfortable and irritable I wanted to scream and then lock myself in a room alone in the dark for an hour afterwards.

Finance, at its basic level, is a real-world application of math. I had the aptitude for both, but leaning on them as my primary means of survival and reason for existing was more than a stretch. Sometimes we have the ability to cultivate a certain skill by expending lots of effort even when the skill itself isn't very compatible with our natural way of being.

If there is any such thing as "finding your passion," I think it has to be something you love doing (the passion part) that is within your primary skill set, something you can do comfortably and effortlessly yet can still continue to grow and improve in the longer you keep at it. Everything is going to take work, but this is where work doesn't seem like "work," you know, the every-day-is-a-grind sort of work. The work takes on phrases with much happier connotations such as "honing your craft." Can I get a do-over?

JOB (IN)SECURITY

MY DAYS as an investment professional didn't always feel compa-
rable to a bad zombie movie. After a year and a half as a bank
examiner post college graduation, I was hired as an investment
performance analyst at a midsize insurance and investment
company. What does that mean? I had no idea at the time either,
but some wonderful people saw potential in me and gave me a
chance. It started as a rather fulfilling career, and most of the
employees' vital signs passed as normal most days, even if the
subject matter wasn't riveting to the average nonzombie.

If you've seen a quarterly statement from some sort of investment account, you probably remember the part where it says
something to the effect of "Your portfolio returned 11.4% for the
quarter." That percentage figure is the work of performance
analysis. The portfolio "performance" was a gain of 11.4%. Of
course, that would be an outstanding positive quarter but not
uncommon during that bull market run we saw in my early days
on the job. Unfortunately, performance isn't always positive, and
we were about to experience some unexpectedly large negative
numbers in the upcoming crisis that would shake the financial
world to its core.

We look at the holdings (stuff you own) and transactions (purchases, sales, dividends, etc.), calculate that little performance number, and then try to "attribute" that performance to various factors within the market. Did interest rates going up help or hurt your portfolio? Did you invest in the energy sector during the oil boom? Did you zig when you should have zagged? The performance number is just that, a number, but the qualitative analysis, the context around that number, is the value we propose to add for our clients.

Prior to my arrival, the company employed a "performance guy" who did all of this work. I was the first person hired as a performance analyst working for the "performance guy." I spent my time learning about the niche of performance measurement and helping him out with the various tasks of the day. About six months into the job, he informed me he was leaving to take another position. Just like that, at the not-so-ripe age of twenty-four, I was essentially a one-man department. The proverbial "sink or swim" moment came rather early in my career.

Now, I wasn't completely alone. My previous boss's manager took over the less technical aspects of his role, but in terms of the expertise of performance measurement, I was it. Still, I was excited by the challenge. I was able to learn things sooner than might happen in most people's careers, and I became a subject matter expert, a "go-to" person at a pretty young age. I took a lot of ownership and pride in my work, sucking it up and figuring out what needed to get done no matter how difficult the project. And a most difficult project was about to befall me.

Perhaps you've seen the movie *The Big Short*? If you have, they actually do an excellent job of explaining what was happening in the investment markets leading up to and during the crash in 2008. If you haven't, I'll try to give you the *small* short according to my limited role in the events that unfolded..

Years ago, the mortgage market was simple. Your bank gave you a mortgage loan, and you paid it back to them over time.

Eventually someone got the idea they could package a bunch of mortgage loans together and sell them as one big asset, a "securitized" asset, a mortgage-backed security.

After that development, instead of banks keeping your mortgage loan in-house after closing, many started selling them to other companies wanting to create these mortgage-backed securities. Your bank then simply serviced the loan, took in your payments, and sent them out to the new owner of your debt while taking a fee for themselves. In that scenario, their biggest moneymaker was the origination fees, what they got paid to initially get you to sign for a mortgage, rather than your ongoing payments. This subtle shift dangled a new carrot, an incentive for increasing the number of mortgage deals overall (quantity over quality), and incentivized banks to overlook credit-worthiness (quality) in order to chase higher short-term profits.

Then investment companies got even cuter, creating derivatives called "credit default swaps." Derivatives are investments that don't have claim to any actual assets themselves but are instead contracts that "derive" their value from the value of a real asset. Credit default swaps were essentially bets (or insurance if used properly and responsibly) on whether or not mortgage-backed securities would fail. If you bought a credit default swap and that specific security did default, you got paid money. In the meantime, the seller of the swap paid you a monthly premium (like insurance) to own the swap contract.

Eventually the market stepped up the complexity with yet another new invention, a deal called a synthetic credit default obligation (a "credit default obligation" is often referred to simply as a "CDO"). A standard credit default obligation is a lot like a mortgage-backed security in that it's basically a pool of a bunch of underlying debt. The synthetic version of this, however, is basically using the credit default swaps we just discussed to "mimic" the performance of a credit default obligation. There is a reason they call this stuff "financial engineering."

A synthetic CDO is inherently riskier than a standard CDO because now you not only have the risk of the CDO defaulting but you also have what they call counterparty risk, the risk that even if you're right in your bet, the company obligated to pay you might not have the money to do so, like a bookie who's broke after a bad weekend of football.

The financial crisis basically amounted to excessive layers of complexity within financial instruments that wound up masking the level of risk involved—or at least making research of risk more challenging—coupled with the greed and hubris of many business folk in the industry. Greed and hubris are ubiquitous, and we all have stories. My early career experience was much more interesting with respect to my behind-the-scenes crash course dealing with the complexity aspect.

A few months before the crisis and market crash, my company decided to invest in one of these synthetic CDO deals with a bigger investment bank on Wall Street (I'll just call them "The Firm"). As you can imagine, considering the size of the deal, this was a huge project and a primary focus for the executives of our company. In order to get in, they had to prove we had a good track record of managing pooled products and credit default swaps and predicting credit risk. As I said, we had been dealing in this market for a while and doing well, but we hadn't been formally tracking our performance on these assets. This became my mandate, and thus began by far the most interesting few months of my career.

I had absolutely no idea what I was getting into. To be fair, neither did most of the investment industry, at least from a performance-calculation perspective. I scrambled to talk with industry experts to understand how to best calculate performance on these newly engineered products, and no one had come up with a concrete method, so we worked together to create a formula. We were traversing a new frontier for my field and the investment industry as a whole.

In parallel, our software didn't have the ability to calculate what it didn't know and understand. I eventually was fortunate enough to get help from one of my friends in IT to build our own proprietary system for this task.

There were no shortages of pressure either. I was reminded of this frequently. For six to eight weeks of my life, I worked from seven in the morning till at least seven at night, sometimes as late as midnight to meet deadlines. It was awful, but it was also oddly thrilling. We were breaking new ground and on the verge of a huge moneymaking deal (so we thought).

I'll be honest, I felt like we did as well as we could have, but given the lack of standards and guidelines, the numbers we put together, though not necessarily flimsy, perhaps didn't have a lot of meaning. I don't know if anyone would say we were being intentionally unethical or misleading, but I felt uneasy providing numbers with a full-throated conviction. We wound up falling back on the motto "When in doubt, disclose." There were a lot of disclosures on our presentations.

When it came time to present to The Firm, I had zero guess as to what their decision might be. As it turned out, they accepted the numbers and signed the deal with us. Three months later, the bottom completely fell out, and our entire company almost went out of business.

I don't know if The Firm had an advantage of asymmetrical information, but one could speculate.

In the midst of all this, most of us spent the better part of the day watching the stock market and the news, wondering what would happen next. If big Wall Street firms like Lehman Brothers, Bear Sterns, and Merrill Lynch were wiped out, certainly we could be too. With each stock that reached near zero, we got more and more nervous. We felt, and hoped, that our Midwest company didn't take on quite as much risk and that our insurance company's capital would keep us afloat.

Soon our closest and biggest competitor down the street got closer and closer to financial ruin. They began announcing layoffs and pay cuts as their stock price cratered over 90%. Despite assurances from management, I started to assume we would at least experience that level of pain. Amazingly, however, we held firm.

Our saving grace wound up being our parent company overseas that had bought us out shortly before I was hired. Since their markets hadn't been hit as hard yet, they had the cushion to keep us afloat. When they did get hit from the financial ripple effect pushing across even vast oceans, they likely had learned enough from the US troubles to avoid the worst-case scenario. By the time the storm was over, we were lucky to have kept everyone on staff without reducing pay (to the best of my knowledge), though the next few years wouldn't show much for raises. Most of us were just grateful to still be employed.

You probably know the rest of the broader story, especially if you watched *The Big Short* or the news at the time. The government went on to regulate these deals to limit risk, but it was too little too late. They bailed out the big Wall Street companies because they were deemed "too big to fail," in other words, too essential to the economy to let them die without ripple effects impacting the rest of us. Unfortunately, much of this bail-out money went to pay large executive bonuses at these firms instead of helping get the average Joe back on his feet after a huge market crash. Wall Street won, and Main Street lost big time.

The events of this crisis got me thinking more about what I wanted out of a career. We all have bills to pay. As a youngster fresh out of college, I needed somewhere to start, and it's flattering for a company to offer you a position. Having cleared that hurdle, however, I learned it was also important for me to evaluate my employer as much as they evaluate me and that those evaluations may evolve over time. I wasn't disillusioned, but I was paying attention and more open to exercising my power of choice.

I also learned a painful lesson on job and income security. Any time I entertained the thought of being self-employed and paving my own path, it always seemed risky and a little irresponsible. Though a corporate job wasn't as secure as I had once thought it to be either. Even if my own performance and reputation was solid in the eyes of management, an entire company could be wiped out overnight.

GRANDPA COMES HOME

"THIS IS MY DUTY," Dad says. "It's time to bring Grandpa home." I don't know if he felt as brave on the inside as he projected on the outside, but I thought it was heroic, almost saint-like. The task he signed up for was incredibly daunting. I know many a family has taken an elder into their home to help care for them, but this seemed different.

Much like with Grandma years ago, Grandpa was suffering from Alzheimer's and/or some form of dementia. In his case, though, it was also paired with Parkinson's disease. The doctors called this deadly combination Lewy body disease. It would probably be a handful for trained professionals at the care center, much less for a family at home. Either way, they had little choice in the matter.

As his condition worsened precipitously, Grandpa's wife, the person he married a few years after Grandma passed, was no longer able to take care of him. The next step would have been a care center, but it was difficult to find available and affordable space on such short notice. Given he was a former marine, he was eligible to be in a VA hospital, but the waiting list was months long.

Dad waited for an opportunity during one of Grandpa's lucid

moments and asked where he wanted to go. I know how proud a man Grandpa was. I can only imagine how difficult it must've been to deal with his disease. He probably wouldn't have asked the question himself, but when Dad posed it to him, he spoke honestly and said he wanted to be with his son.

Fortunately, my stepmom Trish was a trained and licensed nursing professional, and Dad leaned heavily on her skillset. They were able to obtain a hospital bed, which they placed against the wall in the living room adjacent to the bathroom. For a few months' time, that became Grandpa's bedroom.

He had his good days and his bad. At his best, he could climb off the bed and walk on his own to the bathroom. Many days, however, he needed assistance. When he was lucid, his head knew what he wanted to do, but his body didn't always cooperate. I know he was immensely frustrated, but his old-timey, Abbott-and-Costello sense of humor went a long way for him. He would often pump his feet up and down in one place shouting "Okay! Let's go!" but they wouldn't get the proper signals from his brain to move themselves forward. "I'm just revvin' 'em up!" he'd say. "You'd better look out, I'll run ya over!"

He slept a lot, even during the day. I remember it took some getting used to on the days I visited. Everyone else in the house had already grown accustomed to it, including my stepsister Ashley, brother Tyler, and the youngest of the bunch, Nikki. Ashley was Trish's only daughter when she and Dad first got together, and they brought Tyler and Nikki into the world together. What an experience this must have been for everyone. Grandpa would usually wake up a little groggy, perhaps needing some help to sit up and a few minutes to get his wits about him. Then he would notice me.

"HEY!" he'd yell in his silly, staccato way while pointing in my direction. "There he is!"

I remember during one of my visits he was sitting outside on the porch with Dad getting some fresh air. He was in a lawn chair reading a driver's education manual. For obvious reasons, his license had been revoked a year or two before. Dad had asked him some of the things he wanted to do while he was staying there, and he told him he wanted to drive again. Since Dad was the sheriff and worked next door to the DMV office, he was able to bring home a manual for Grandpa to study. Every day Dad would tell him he could take the test next week.

"I'm studying for the test, Brett. I'm gonna get back there on the road soon, so watch out!"

He would look over a page for a few minutes, then talk to me for a while and make conversation, sometimes circling back to the fact that he was getting his license again, then go back to studying the same page for a few minutes more.

All the times I saw him at Dad's place, he never wore his Sunday clothes. No slacks, no button-up shirts. He spent most of his time in T-shirt and sweatpants, or sometimes just boxer shorts if he forgot the sweatpants. He rarely ever talked about church anymore. I assume a lot of that faded away with the disease. It was sad to see the things he couldn't do, but it was also heartening to watch him accept certain realities and just let go. Who cared if he forgot your name? Who cared if he was sitting around in his boxer shorts reading a drivers' education manual?

He was just living. And he was happy to be there. We were all happy to have the time with him.

I wasn't there during the tougher moments, however. I didn't have to help him eat or go to the bathroom. I wasn't there to witness some of the worst dementia episodes, the night terrors he would have, the times he fought against Dad and Trish as they tried to help him. I didn't have to help change his clothes, help bathe him, or help clean things up on his worst days. I didn't have to worry about his heart and his atrial fibrillation or whether or not I would need to rush him to the hospital. But they did. Every day.

I remember sitting at home afterward, sick with guilt and shame, wondering whether I would have the balls to do what

Dad was doing if we were in the same situation thirty years down the road. When I envisioned such a scenario, my first thoughts weren't "Of course, I can do this. It's my dad. I'd step up" but rather "I don't know if I can do this. I don't know if I'm strong enough." And then I would just sit there, afraid and ashamed.

Maybe you just have to be put in the situation first before you know how you would react. I suppose it's all speculation until the day arrives. Maybe Dad was afraid too. Maybe he didn't know if he could do it. Maybe part of him even didn't want to do it, but he just had to and he found a way. If I'm ever faced with a similar challenge, I can only hope to be half that brave.

I think deep down what really scares me is the possibility of losing Dad. Not only the ultimate loss, but the prelude, losing who he really is while he's still alive. I remember talking to Dad on the porch about Grandpa. You rarely see Dad's strife on display, his Teflon armor always shielding the rest of the world from what's inside, but that day there were some visible cracks.

"He was my freaking idol, Brett. There was nothing he couldn't do. It's just really tough to see him this way." I didn't have any answers. We sat in silence, letting the words breathe. He was saying things of his father that were true about him for me. Surely, he knew. I assumed he knew.

I know these neurological diseases can be genetic. Now that Grandpa and Grandma have both been torn down from the inside out, I shudder at the thought of seeing it again. I don't want Dad to have to deal with that during the last few years of his life, to have to go out that way. It steals your dignity before it takes your life. I don't want to wake up and realize the dad I knew is gone and feel cheated out of moments I had thought were still coming. It happened so insidiously with my grandparents.

There were still things I wanted to ask Grandpa, but I had lost my opportunity. I wanted to talk to him about God and religion and ask him how he was able to believe the things I am unable to. Now as a free-thinking adult myself, I understand some of the appeal of religion and Christianity, but I also see how some of it may simply be a story we tell ourselves to make peace with the inevitability of death. Death still scares the shit out of me, and it would be great if there were an afterlife, but my faith in one seems unlikely to affect the outcome. I find that it is more honest and humbling for me to admit that I'm only human, and so I don't know, and that's okay. If there is a God—and they are good—I can't fathom how this being would punish us for ignorance or curiosity.

Selfishly I worry about meeting my end as a shell of my former self too. Every time I wander into a room and can't remember why, or I reach for a word I can't find, I wonder, "Is this how it starts?" When I miss a step walking up the stairs or clumsily drop a plate while unloading the dishwasher, I wonder, "Is this what Parkinson's feels like?" Sometimes when I bend down to reach for something and it feels awkward or painful, it reminds me of how I used to see Grandpa move. I start to wonder if I'm just getting older or if it's an early sign of Parkinson's. I can feel in myself what I saw in him. I do something and think, "That felt like Grandpa looked." Of course it did, he's my grandpa, and those are my genes, but is there another reason this seems familiar?

I think that's why I always keep moving, because I'm afraid if I stop it might be hard to get started again. I'm afraid of what I feel creeping in while sitting in my office chair hour after hour after hour. I don't know if these thoughts are irrational or not.

There's apparently a genetic test you can take that isolates a particular gene indicating high likelihood of Alzheimer's. Neither Dad nor Bevan, nor their sister, my aunt Bobbi, has chosen to take it. I can't blame them. Would I want to know? If you had the ability to see your fate, would you want to know? Would it empower you to do things differently, or, if bad news, would it sentence you to a life of fear, dreading the inevitable? Alzheimer's is like a ticking time bomb just waiting to go off;

would you want to see the clock or be blissfully ignorant of its existence? I suppose we all have some sort of clock anyway.

I've heard Dad and Bevan refer to a pact they have in the event they find out they drew the wrong genetic cards—an injection of a sweet, sweet sleep serum. I don't know if it's a joke or not. They might not know, either. I wouldn't be surprised if part of their motivation would simply be to prevent others from having to take care of them in this way, that they are trying to learn from their past experiences.

True or not, it wouldn't be out of character. Dad's first instinct is always kids first, him last. Extreme? Yes. Out of character? No. If I had the ability to see into the future, but I could only pick one event, I wouldn't use it to know if I myself develop Alzheimer's. I'd use it to see whether or not my dad did, how I dealt with it, and whether I learned anything.

Dad and Grandpa while we
were fishing in Canada my
sophomore year of college. I've
purchased two disposable
cameras in my life, and I'm
glad I used this one.

GRANDPA WANTS YOU TO BE HAPPY

WHILE WORKING through some mildly important spreadsheet at my desk, I was interrupted by iPhone vibrations. Peeking out the corner of my peripheral, I saw my dad's name on the caller ID. I didn't remember him ever calling while I was at work. The weight of the reality I expected was already immense before even answering the phone.

After a few months of staying at my old house with Dad, Grandpa had finally landed an open room at the nursing home in Luverne, Minnesota, the same facility where Grandma lived out her final days. Those images of hallways, room numbers, name plates, and hospital beds flew through my mind as I suspected that was the location from which Dad was calling.

I grabbed the phone and ran toward a conference room, answering it halfway to the door. Before he even spoke, I heard sniffs and knew my dad had tears in his eyes. And then so did I.

"This is the end, Brett. We are in the home with him. There are probably only a few hours left. He's in a coma, but the doctors think he can still hear us. If you would like to see him, you need to come soon."

Here I was, a grown-ass man in a corporate office building, bawling like a child. I had yet to speak at this point, but I was making sounds. He then asked me, "Do you want to come see him?"

I had so many thoughts rushing through my head. Historically speaking, I had made some tough decisions favoring company over family. I usually used the stress and the so-called importance of work as an excuse to dodge some familial responsibility. As the oldest child with some much younger siblings, I occasionally slipped into old habit and waited for my parents to tell us—and by extension, me—I had to do something rather than actively choose. Such decisions usually led to future regret.

As Dad awaited a response, my mind instinctively began formulating the reasons not to go until something inside me started to push back. Likely sensing my tension and conflict in the silence, Dad spoke again.

"I have absolutely no expectations of you, Son. I just want to give you the opportunity. I love you and understand no matter what choice you make."

I wasn't going to let myself regret this one.

"I want to come."

"Promise me something before you decide to come," he said. "You have to promise me you are emotionally ready for a four-hour drive. I know this can be a lot to take in, and the last thing I want to do is have you get in an accident as a distracted driver. I know you want to come, and he would love you to, but we have to make a quick, logical decision right now, okay?"

My dad worked for a number of years as a deputy sheriff, an undercover investigator, and eventually as sheriff. He was a natural at handling himself and others during moments of trauma. We came to our final decision, and he got me into the right frame of mind to make the trip. Just hearing his voice and his logical way of walking me through the process was enough. Most often, in times of distress, all I need is a phone call from Dad.

After hanging up the phone and wiping a few tears, I calmly walked back to my boss's desk and invited him to a conference room. I told him what was going on, and I said I needed a week. Within an hour I was packed and heading to the nursing home. Of course, there were no guarantees he'd still be breathing when I arrived.

It's rather amazing how your mind finds a way to compartmentalize when it needs to focus. I thought about a lot during those four hours as I drove straight through to Luverne, Minnesota, but I never really got emotional. None of my dad's concerns came to pass, thankfully. I was steady and calm and drove as efficiently as I had ever driven in my life. Thankfully, I wasn't too late. The next thing I remember was meeting Dad outside the nursing home as he chaperoned me to Grandpa's room.

When I got there, a number of my other family members were sitting in chairs around the room. Grandpa was lying in bed breathing choppily and, at times, gasping. His eyes were closed, and the only thing moving was his chest, up and down. None of us knew if another inhalation would follow the last exhalation. I'd never watched someone die before, and the imminence of it was overwhelming. The juxtaposition of something so common yet so feared left me feeling unprepared for the moment. Death is the most reliable of human occurrences, yet I'd never felt so unprepared for any single moment in my life.

Dad again reminded me that, though Grandpa did not appear to be totally awake, the doctors did have reason to believe he could hear what we were saying. He asked me if I wanted to talk. I walked over to the bed and grabbed his hand much like I would a small child's—despite its massive size—sandwiching it between my own two palms.

It then became apparent most of my family was watching me have a moment with my grandfather, which transported me into my childhood body in an instant. I was a rather shy kid, and everyone in the room knew that about me. Even though I had come out of my shell somewhat as an adult, somehow familial situations have a way of pulling you back into old patterns.

Through some quick inner dialogue, I convinced myself this was a transcendent moment.

I looked him in the eyes, just in case he might open them, and said, "I don't know if you waited for me, but if you did, I'm glad." Much like any of my public speaking engagements in grade school or middle school, the rest of my words were a blur, but I do remember closing with "I love you, Grandpa."

I felt helpless not knowing whether he heard me. Even if he had, I don't know if he would've understood. The last time I had seen him in the home, it had been all but impossible to engage in a meaningful discussion.

That last visit had been on his birthday, and we had wheeled him outside on the patio to celebrate and give him a card. His misfiring brain got very nervous about the pace of the card opening. He frantically cried at us to open it faster, as if something terrible would happen if we didn't, all the while kicking the foot supports of his wheelchair much like a toddler would a stroller during a fit. All you can do is remind yourself that the disease has control; it's no longer them.

After I spoke my piece, we all sat around Grandpa's bedside telling stories into the evening until, one by one, we filtered out to get home and rest ourselves. We agreed Dad would be the first one back in at seven o'clock the following morning. As it turned out, when he arrived the next day, he was about ten minutes too late.

A nurse was in the process of cleaning Grandpa for the day. She stepped out of the room briefly to get some supplies, and when she returned, his soul had passed. Everyone in the family thought it was so fitting he would wait until he was alone for his last moment. Always the caretaker, and never short on pride, I suppose he didn't want anyone to bear the burden of watching.

I spent the next few days before the funeral reminiscing with my family. At the time, I was in a relationship with a woman named Amber, and it had become complicated emotionally and logistically. I wasn't sure what the future held for us, but she asked me if I wanted her to come, and I said yes. I figured this was no time for working through relationship conflicts, and I was appreciative of her support and presence.

As sad as it was to say goodbye, everyone in the family marveled at how wonderful the ceremony was. Bevan, Brandon, and my cousin Travis are all fantastic singers, and they put on a wonderful show in remembrance of Pastor B. As we traveled to the gravesite, I was fortunate to be able to play my guitar while Dad said his last words to the tunes of "Wonderful Life" and "Watch Over You." Then he looked up to the sky as he pictured Grandpa dancing with Grandma once again. I'm sure neither of them had ever listened to Alter Bridge, but I hope they enjoyed the offering and perhaps found the rhythm.

A couple months down the road, as my struggles with Amber became more serious, some things were said that I must assume were driven by emotion. She lived more than two hours from me and had two children. I had mostly moved in with them perhaps eight or ten months prior to the funeral as we had both looked forward to merging our lives together. In the exciting early stages of the relationship, nothing else seemed to matter. I thought I was more than capable of compromising for the sake of being with "the one." As the initial bliss faded to daily life, however, I became restless with having uprooted my life. It's surprising how your vision adjusts when emotions level off.

At first I found it difficult to be honest with myself as I slowly grew more aware of just how much I had willingly compromised. I didn't want to think I'd made the wrong deci-sion or admit I didn't understand myself and my needs as well as I thought I did. Then I found it difficult being honest with Amber until it came to the point where it was impossible for me to keep my feelings inside. The hardest part was finding the right words, until one succinct phrase occurred to me that captured my situation just about as well as anything could.

"I feel like a fish out of water," I told her. I felt so far away from everything that was "home" to me that I had no idea how to build a new one or where to even begin. I had chosen to join the ride as a passenger in her life without thinking how I might make it my own. Our own.

At the time I moved in with her, I was still working for my same investment company, three weeks remotely from her house and one week onsite. Each week I spent at the office and at my old home—a condo where I roomed with a longtime buddy from college—I found it harder to make the trip back. Which was ironic because when Amber and I were dating long distance, each time one of us left the other, we couldn't wait until the next time we were together.

I missed her, but I also didn't know how to make the rest of the pieces fit. At the same time, I didn't know how we would continue to work on our relationship if we went back to the long-distance scenario. The effort was too daunting, and what would be the point if I couldn't see moving at a future date? Likewise, her moving my direction with her kids was off the table, and I wouldn't have felt good about that either.

Perhaps the most frustrating part was knowing I wasn't happy but not knowing in the affirmative what I actually did want in order to change that. Was it about me not knowing if I wanted children? Was it uncertainty toward her as the right partner? Was it about being in a new city or being forced to inevitably find a new job (I was already questioning my current one anyway)? The incompleteness of my thoughts left me unsatisfied, and it was likely more unsatisfying to her.

Every foundational pillar of my life seemed to come into question at the same time: my spirituality, my love life, my career, my very identity itself. Instead of being able to reason and work through it all, my brain was stuck on an infinite loop always winding up at a dead end until it simply shut down.

I spent much of this time guilty and upset with myself for both not initially acknowledging these obstacles for what they were and for somehow being unwilling or unable to make the sacrifice that I used to think was the proper romantic thing to do. To her credit, she briefly voiced concern about this very possibility in the early weeks of our relationship. She said she even contemplated ending our relationship when it was only a few weeks old because she was afraid of, as she put it, complicating my life. Perhaps this subconsciously drove me to prove that it wouldn't. What I did understand at the time was that I wouldn't know what would happen if I didn't try.

The future had proved her to be the more accurate prognosticator. Nevertheless, when it played out the way it did, I couldn't help but be frustrated she didn't show more sympathy for my inner conflict. I don't know if it would have changed the outcome, but I still longed for some level of compassion to help me through. I know she wanted me to be happy there with her, but I couldn't force it either. I started to feel emotional distance grow to match our geographical distance. The more I pulled away, the harder she tried to hold on to what we had. In the process, she made one very unfortunate comment, wielding her perception of my grandpa's spirit as a blunt object.

"What about your grandfather?" she said. "He was a great family man. If he were still here, he would be telling you to make this work."

For a moment, I literally could not believe the words I had heard. I knew the statement was completely unfair, completely speculative, and that she didn't know my grandfather from Adam. Still, in the heat of the moment, it was extremely hard to shake.

After the breakup, I had a number of counseling sessions with my dad (in addition to formal sessions with a licensed professional). We had covered a lot of ground, but I hadn't mentioned this one particular comment yet. I don't know if I was trying to show how out of line she was or if I really wondered whether or not it was true, but I needed to ask Dad his opinion on the matter.

"She said what?"

"She said Grandpa would have told me to make it work, that family comes first."

Dad's face contorted into the most quizzical of expressions as if fighting off a brain cramp. I'm not sure if he was trying to process her statement, question why I was concerned about it, both, or something else. But he said, "If Grandpa were alive, he'd simply tell you to do what makes you happy."

I remind myself of this any time I have a tough decision to make. There's a difference between being selfish and being true to oneself. I have often found it hard to strike the right balance and learned some painful lessons along the way. Still, I think it's a worthy pursuit.

BREW 'N POO (AND OTHER "GREAT" IDEAS)

A HANDFUL OF YEARS AGO, on a seemingly irresponsible whim, Brandon moved to San Francisco. He was tired of his first career path in criminal justice and corrections and was looking for a change. He didn't have shit for money and couldn't bring much in the way of personal belongings in his little Camry, so he started selling his stuff, even things I thought he'd never part with. I purchased his Taylor guitar because I couldn't bear to see it leave the family. He has since purchased it back, which, I must admit, was my hope from the outset.

He didn't even have a job lined up when he left, just an apartment. This was always a major difference between the two of us; he was far more spontaneous, driven by his own curious instinct. I preferred to have a logical, concrete plan in place before making any big life decisions.

His first idea in terms of income generation was the possibility of getting into dog walking. Apparently, there was pretty good business walking wealthier and busier people's dogs out in San Francisco. There was even an app for it. The business model sounded a lot like puppy Uber.

What he ultimately wound up doing, however, was getting a job at a SoulCycle studio, a spin class franchise blowing up in the larger metro areas. It didn't seem like a bad gig, but wasn't exactly a high-paying one either. He started small and eventually worked his way up to what I would call an operations manager, taking care of budgeting and scheduling. I think he also got to take a few classes for free, if memory serves, which aren't exactly cheap. Nice perk, I suppose.

He became quite fond of the business, the job, and his coworker friends, but the pay was not enough to make ends meet, even with a roommate or two. Such is the plight of many a millennial living in a big coastal city these days. After a little more than a year, he was forced to admit it was over and return home, chalking the whole thing up as a life experience.

The times we talked upon his return, he still seemed to have a breath of refreshing California air rolling over his vocal cords. He had an idea. He wanted to start his own cycling studio.

My brother has a lot of ideas, which is a good thing because somebody has to come up with them. The first one that comes to mind is Brew & Poo, a coffee house with top-notch java and immaculately pristine bathrooms. There was also some sort of laundry contraption; you could directly transfer the entire load from the washer to the dryer in one shot. His track record of following through, however, has not been great. While eager to hear him out on his latest idea of the month, I honestly had pretty low expectations.

Once he opened his mouth, though, I was pleasantly surprised with what came out. He had a fairly extensive and well-written business plan. He had also run some numbers and put together a solid budget, less surprising since this was a big part of his job at SoulCycle. It was like watching my little brother grow up right before my eyes. He began some due diligence, evaluating nearby places where he could make this work. He was coming up with logos and thoughts about how to run the classes and what other amenities could possibly be included to supplement cycling.

For a period of weeks, if someone had asked me to bet, I

would've put money on him filing papers, and I still think there was a good chance he could've made this work. As it happened, though, he started to waver on the idea. He started to lose some confidence and second-guess himself. And then he reached out to other more senior family members for advice on the matter.

He queried our uncle Bevan, who was an advertising executive at a large retail company on the east coast. Smart choice on my brother's part. I came to learn of this conversation through my dad when the two of us were talking about Brandon's idea. My dad is a smart man, both for the things he knows as well as for understanding his limits. Business and marketing are more in his brother's wheelhouse, so he deferred and put a lot of stock in Bevan's opinion.

My dad opens with Bevan's most prescient comment: "Brandon needs to figure out who he is first. And if he really wants to do this, he needs to go in one hundred percent."

My brother had been talking about starting small, perhaps even doing this as a side business first while having another paycheck-based occupation in parallel. Then, if the business grew, he would go from his initial small-view idea and start to incorporate the bigger-view ideas as he faded away from his day job. On the one hand, this seems very practical, but in our uncle's opinion, it was a recipe for failure. If you have a fallback plan, you're likely to use it.

Bevan is a wise sage, and not only because of his snowy-white, Santa-esque beard and super-sharp modern glasses. He's been in the marketing and advertising business for decades and clearly is doing something right to be where he is within his organization. The only way he knew to go was all in, one hundred percent.

The catch is you can't go all in on something that isn't truly aligned with who you are. I mean, literally, it's not possible. That's where your conscience starts to pull you back to your fallback plan as it convinces you to justify the move with words like "practical" and "sensible."

Of all the people in my life who could speak to the idea of truly understanding who they are as a person, Bevan would have to have the most street cred. First of all, he decided to grow that beard on purpose and actually goes out in public that way. Second of all, he was a gay man born and raised in the heart of conservative, rural Iowa, son of a First Reformed Church minister.

Even now, but especially during Bevan's younger years in the 1970s, the world can give you a thousand reasons to not be open about your homosexuality. I'm sure moving to New York made things somewhat easier, but I will never fully appreciate the existential crisis he and others like him most certainly went through.

When my brother and I went to visit him (and, of course, the beach) when I was around age twelve, he had a roommate, Antonio. Of course he had a roommate. It's New York. The place is fucking expensive. Antonio was a super cool guy, super friendly, and we had a blast rollerblading with him through Battery Park. Bevan also had a dog. I don't remember the name, but I think it was a miniature pincher perhaps?

At one point Brandon and I were sitting in the living room watching TV or eating lunchables or doing whatever kids do, and Bevan asked Antonio if he had let the dog out yet that afternoon. At least that's all I heard. After they left the room, Brandon looked at me with big old moon eyes and said, "Did you hear that?"

"Hear what?"

"Bevan called Antonio 'Honey!'"

"Seriously?"

"Yeah!"

At some point after the trip, Brandon worked up the courage to ask Dad about the "Honey" comment. Dad sat us down and explained to us our uncle liked men.

I was surprised for sure, simply because I hadn't before known anyone who was openly gay. Still, it seemed simple enough to me: he liked guys. End of story. No big deal.

But then I started to recall my experiences at school and what I had seen on TV. I thought to myself, "Why do my friends use 'gay' as a derogatory term? Why do kids in school call me 'gay' when they are trying to make fun of me or if they don't like me?" I had also heard people from church mutter about how the Bible called out homosexuality and how God was against it, or something to that effect.

At first, I was confused, wondering who was in the "right" here. And then I felt guilty for entertaining the prejudiced ideas the people in my community had put in my head. For the first time I can remember, I started to entertain the idea that perhaps there wasn't a "right" or "wrong." Maybe life is a little more complicated. Also, I loved my uncle.

I became overwhelmed with empathy for Bevan. I tried to put myself in his shoes and wondered what it must be like to deal with such crap, people not only making fun of you but perhaps also thinking less of you as a human being.

A few weeks later, I received a letter from my uncle. To this day, I wish I had saved it, but I can remember how it began:

"My dearest nephew, I am flying on a plane thousands of feet in the air, and I felt compelled to write you."

My uncle never lacks in sophistication and formality.

With that letter, I felt as though I had a special bond with my uncle. It made us feel closer, him willing to open up to me about a difficult subject. I also thought he was pretty cool at the time for using words like "compelled." Likewise, as I got older, I came to appreciate his knack for using the English language more broadly. Though I don't get to see my uncle very often, the geography and his travel schedule being the biggest obstacles, I always treasure the times we do have together. In between, though admittedly not as often as I ought to, I write to him just as he once wrote to me. I know the words I'll receive back will be void of fluff, filtered down to pure, white-bearded wisdom.

As it turns out, building a SoulCycle-like business was not who Brandon was. He liked the idea of it, and I think he was excited about the creative process and the prospects of having his own business, but it didn't swim in his veins the way it needed to for him to dedicate his life to it, even if only for a few years until something else came along.

Sometime later, he began talking more about the prospects of becoming a fishing guide. It was on the heels of a trip he took to the boundary waters in Minnesota, and Dad and I jointly owned our boat by this time, so it was an enticing and also potentially realistic discussion to have for any one of us.

Dad had also raised this idea as something he could do either part-time or full-time if he decided to leave the machining job he took while in retirement as a former sheriff. Personally, I enjoyed the discussions and was excited about them, but it was a more vicarious excitement for me; I was on the outside looking in as an investment professional.

After posting pictures of our fishing vacations on social media, Dad had been getting many inquiries from people at his workplace and friends around town about taking them fishing. They even started offering him money, saying they had looked up rates for other guides and felt they'd be willing to pay the same or similar. How wonderful it would be, right? Fish every day for a living? That would be the life!

Those discussions, benign as they seemed to me personally at the time, burrowed deep into my brain and began making plans for my future, unbeknownst to me. They took advantage of my struggles and frustrations with the corporate office environment, slowly infiltrating, one neuron at a time, until I began thinking about the prospect more seriously myself.

HYPNOSIS AND FORGIVENESS

I HAD THOUGHT I'd made peace with the divorce scene all those years ago until it invited itself into a hypnotherapy session. My physical therapist had recommended hypnosis as a treatment for a nervous system on high alert and afraid to move its body for fear of pain. The hypnotist could theoretically tap into that fear within the subconscious to release past traumas and help get me "unstuck." He probably meant unstuck physically, but I was about to get into some emotional stickiness. Perhaps it's all the same, or at least related.

I had run the tape of the divorce moment so many times in my head I could have directed the movie if there was one, at least up to the moment it cuts off. I thought I'd gleaned every last piece of info and learned every last lesson to be learned years ago, so the VHS labeled "The Divorce" sat dusty on a shelf in the archives of my brain alongside other well-worn titles like "First Day of School" and "Swallowed Dad's Chew Spit and Ashes Thinking They Were Mountain Dew." It almost seemed silly to even bother talking about it again, but I went along with it.

The scene opens with my return home from a day of school as a first or second grader. I set down my backpack on the old steam radiator just inside the door. Dad was there, not so much to greet me as to usher me toward something. Mom was in the living room sitting anxiously on our couch. Dad called my brother and asked us both to sit near Mom because she had something to tell us.

I immediately sensed trouble. The hair stood at attention on the back of my neck, my stomach turned, and my body shook with worry. I had been hoping to get home and play Super Mario Brothers. Whatever was waiting for us on the couch was anything but a game.

Mom clearly didn't want to be doing this either. She looked very uncomfortable, almost as if she were sitting in a stranger's house. The formality of the ordeal made me feel like a stranger there too.

Months before this discussion, our Aunt Karla, mom's twin sister, had divorced our Uncle Kevin. Upon hearing the news, I sprinted up to my room, where I cried for an hour in bed. Perhaps I cared that much about my aunt and uncle. Or perhaps I cared immensely, at age seven, about the sanctity of marriage? Doubtful. I think subconsciously I knew how alike the twins were. I feared Mom might do the same.

Back then, it was my mom who was consoling me in my bedroom. She tried to explain why my aunt and uncle were getting divorced and why things were different for her. As we sat on the couch with mom this time, tears began to form in my eyes again as I suspected different words this time around.

"I'm going to live with Karla for a while," she said a bit unsteadily but matter of factly.

"I want you guys to live here so you can stay in the same house and so, Brett, you can go to your same school."

I had to question whether or not that was the truth or if she just didn't want to bring us with her. I think any child could be forgiven for pondering such a question, but I never vocalized it.

I remember my brother switching his gaze toward Mom one moment, me the next, trying to understand what was going on.

I'm sure at his age of three he didn't comprehend the meaning or the gravity of the situation, but he definitely inferred I was not happy about it. Either reflexively or in sympathy, he started to cry too.

I have to imagine the conversation continued longer, but that's where the tape cuts. It's almost as if I blacked out from that point forward until we first visited her in the new apartment. Psychologists will tell you memory pulls this trick to protect a person.

As I revisited this scene under hypnosis, I could sense a subtle shift in perspective. At the time I was living it, I saw her as a mean mommy leaving and hurting her kids. That view softened a lot over the following months and years, certainly, but subconsciously I may have been holding on to more than I realized. This time, however, as I continued to hold that scene in my mind, carefully studying my mom's face, expressions, and body language, all I saw was a scared little thirteen-year-old girl frozen in time from the moment she learned her dad was killed in a snowmobile accident and now panicking and confused as to what to do with her life, what to do with a marriage she wasn't prepared for, and whether or not she could be true to herself while minimizing collateral damage to her kids. Perhaps all the pillars of her life had come into question at the same time; I could relate to that. Part of me let go a little.

I suppose this is what forgiveness feels like. I thought I had already forgiven her, at least that's what I had told myself and others. Perhaps forgiveness happens only gradually and sometimes even imperceptibly. My brother and I had talked about it at length with Dad every night before bed for the better part of a year. "Can we talk about Mom?" one of us would say as he tucked us into bed. After perhaps a year, it became an obvious bedtime stalling mechanism, and Dad eventually caught on to us, but the first many nights it was very much a necessity.

As we grew older, I would still occasionally have one-off conversations, trying to fill in some of the pieces with either

Dad or Brandon. And yes, I had talked directly with my mom about it, though not as frequently. I probably should have asked her more, but I always lacked the courage to raise the issue. It likely would have accelerated the healing process. I don't know if what I let go during this hypnosis session was the rest of my grief, nor do I know what it should feel like if that were the case. My reflections and writing thereafter did open the door for Mom and I to have some of the deepest conversations we've ever had on the subject, though, which has to be a good thing.

As a young child, the divorce felt like a broken promise and instilled a lack of trust at an early age. But I now understand that nothing is guaranteed, and loss is a part of life from which you can't insulate yourself. Sometimes you get hurt, but forgiveness is a powerful tool. And if you don't take any chances, you'll never experience any of the rewards. In other words, life happens, and we get through it. Letting go of the past can leave you open to a brighter future.

Mom's fish and a major source
of jealousy. Speaking of which,
you should be jealous of my
short shorts and that Batman
t-shirt.

GIRLS JUST WANNA HAVE FUN

A FEW YEARS after the divorce, my brother and I were spending a weekend with Mom and our stepdad, Bruce. We were playing some sort of loosely organized question-and-answer game we made up, and someone asked Mom, "What song most describes you?"

"I'm like Cyndi Lauper: I just wanna have fun!"

At the time it was a silly, throw-away comment in a made-up game we played, but for some reason it stuck with me, and I've thought about it more over the years. I do think it says something about her, and it could go one of two ways. When confronted with the most difficult aspects of life, she diverts, she chooses just to have fun. Or, in spite of all the challenges thrown her way, she still somehow manages to have fun. Both may be true. She is admittedly averse to conflict, yet it is often argued that laughter and a light-hearted approach to life are effective coping mechanisms that can lead to a long and happy life.

If you want to win my mom over, you simply need to dance with her and make her laugh. If you can't make her laugh yourself, taking her to a stand-up comedy show is a great substitute. She's most definitely a giggler, an infectious and uncontrollable giggler, especially when she's drinking, but even when she's not. She probably just read that as "she's *snot*" and started laughing by herself, leaving those around her to ask what the hell is going on. Any one of us could accidentally read the same words in that way, but she is unique in her capacity to laugh at her mistakes and is refreshingly willing to indulge in the occasional bit of silly, child-like humor.

My stepdad nearly blew it with the first of these two items when they initially met. She approached him first and told him to dance with her, and he said "no thanks" because he's "not much of a dancer." She called him an asshole and walked away. Somehow, they worked it out from there and got married a couple years later.

Much like with Dad and Trish, it was initially hard for me to accept the idea of Mom moving on, but Bruce is a pretty damn good guy. He also made it clear from the start he was not there to replace my dad but rather to be a friend and a support system, probably the best thing he could've done to win me over. Building a one-acre farm pond and stocking it with fish didn't hurt either.

Still, it was a process. A few months after the wedding, during one of our visits to Mom and Bruce's house, Mom stat us down on the couch again. There were eerie parallels, but at least it was a different couch this time, and I didn't have the same level of trepidation.

"I have some news, boys," she said with an anxious smile. "You're going to have a little baby sister!"

I lost my shit. I crumpled to the ground as if I had suddenly been afflicted with a massive neuromuscular condition and began spewing tears all over the living room carpet. Whatever condition this was didn't affect my vocal cords or tear ducts in the least.

My emotions had nothing to do with my future sister at all; I was struck by the finality of my changing family. I had recently learned that marriage could be temporary, but I inherently knew babies were much less so. Mom and Dad certainly weren't getting back together now.

After a few minutes of crying and coming to terms with the situation, I felt better. Mom and I began to talk about our future sister, Taylor Marie, and I slowly started shifting into excitement mode. Having a sister would be a neat new experience. Mom told me I could change her diapers, and somehow this chore made me feel like a proud big brother, and I started looking forward to the role.

Unfortunately, my actions had set off a wicked domino effect. Once Brando took his cue from his older brother that this was a thing we didn't want, he went to work. He ran and hid behind the banister between the living room and the kitchen as Mom and I talked on the couch. Later we heard him shuffling across the floor and digging in the drawers at the counter. At this point the shock factor had settled down for me enough to notice the hilarity of the situation.

Eventually a crumpled napkin hurtled toward the couch from the other side of the banister. I picked it up and opened it. Brandon had been writing.

"We hat the babee!"

Mom and I started laughing so hard our stomachs hurt. Then came another.

"Deth to the babee!"

Now Mom and I had to get Brandon under control, and I had to clean up my mess.

"I'm not sad, Brandon. I was just surprised. It's okay now."

Thankfully, learning about Teryn's pending birth a few years later was much less traumatic. When that second pregnancy was announced, we took it in stride and had another good laugh at Brandon's antics over Taylor.

Mom is pretty good at making other people laugh, too, but not in the traditional jokester sort of way. It's usually more in the "Moooooom, you're embarrassing me!" sort of way. Often she interprets the world missing one key observation, and this leaves you shaking your head, yet you can't help but laugh. I hope she knows we're always laughing *with* her. Most of the time she does, and her aforementioned ability to laugh at herself is a wonderful tool for life survival. You either own it or it owns you.

Also, when she's joined by her partner-in-crime, twin sister Karla, the silliness can multiply exponentially. Even their names, Marla and Karla, seem to beg for a TV sitcom, *The 'Arlas*. They always claim they have a lost sister Darla somewhere out in the world, and I imagine that would be one of the storylines that would carry the show.

Mom has frequently prodded me to write a book about her Marla-isms, and while this book is certainly not dedicated solely to that request, I'll divulge the one our family remembers most fondly.

A number of years ago, she and Bruce took a trip to Las Vegas and met another couple who were sporting a car with a Hawaii license plate. She immediately blurted out, "Oh my God! Did you drive here?!" Ironically, part of the reason for visiting Las Vegas was to see Bill Engvall's show "Here's Your Sign," a response the comedian developed to reply to people asking stupid questions, it being his view that all such people ought to wear a sign saying "I'm stupid" so no one relies on them or asks them anything.

Mom has had a number of hilarious "here's-your-sign" moments throughout her life, and she has mostly laughed through all of them. Lest you think she is offended by any "here's-your-sign" jokes, you should know Bill Engvall is one of her favorite comedians of all time.

Mom is an extreme people pleaser, and I suspect this is part of the reason she is so comfortable laughing at herself. If we are laughing, we are having fun, and that's all she wants. Once she knows we're all having fun, then she can relax. In fact, she has stated numerous times that she doesn't want a funeral but rather a celebration when she passes. She envisions looking down on everyone laughing and smiling and telling stories about her life rather than crying and wallowing in sadness.

The first funeral she ever attended was her father's, and it was anything but the kind she hopes for when she passes. A cele-bration of life would have been a difficult sell at such a young age and given the tragic circumstances of her father's accident. Knowing how much I treasure the relationship with my own dad, I can't even imagine the extent to which this changed the course of her life.

When Mom left my dad (and, as it seemed to me at the time, my brother and me as well), I struggled hard to process it. It seemed as though we were not part of her Cyndi Lauper version of fun, but there was so much I couldn't understand at that age. Had she truly left because she just wanted to have more fun, or did she simply feel pressured by society to rush into a family and this was her first bold move to reclaim her own authenticity?

Either way, you can't make decisions without consequences; but you also can't continue moving down a given path once you've concluded it is not your truest one. It was a painful way to learn such a lesson, yet I still have to give my mom credit for teaching it to me in her own indirect way. Dad is direct. Mom is the opposite. Her "teaching" typically leaves a few mysterious puzzle pieces for me to put together over time before I under-stand what I am supposed to take away from it.

Looking back, this was the best route for our family to go. Or maybe I just can't see it any other way now. She moved, but it's not fair to say she abandoned us. She loved us. She was proud of us and bragged about us incessantly to anyone who would listen. She took us fun places and tried, to the extent she was financially able, to give us things we would enjoy.

Immediately after the divorce, she didn't yet have the resources to buy fancy toys we wanted from a magazine or a TV commercial, so inevitably she entertained us more with activi-ties, playing tennis at the park or hanging out near a little stream that ran behind her apartment complex. Those memories lasted longer and feel warmer than anything money could have purchased.

At one point she did, however, buy me a pet snake. I had asked Dad first, but he had told me "no" after our bad experience with an Amazon tree boa, not at all the friendly companion the traditional boa constrictor is. We kept it in a cage and filmed National Geographic-style videos of it hammering the glass and destroying gerbils until it choked on one that was apparently too large and Dad returned it. The thing coiled up on his glove so hard I was worried he wouldn't get it off. When we got to the pet store, the manager who was working the desk that particular day said, "Did you have that thing with those two little boys over there? They shouldn't have sold you this snake."

So, Mom bought us this little fox snake—which I ever so creatively named "Foxy"—not knowing Dad didn't want one in the house. I heard him raising his voice at Mom until I stepped in and said I had asked her to. I don't remember that conversation ending well, but we did keep Foxy for a while, and he too wound up choking on his food—frozen dead mice that the same pet store upgraded in size too quickly—and wound up kicking the bucket. We buried him out back by the garage next to our former iguana, Iggy.

She always supported our education and our creative endeavors as well as our career choices. She drove hours to watch many of my basketball and football games, even if she did happen to be in the bathroom when I scored my first touchdown. That's just rotten luck. I am more sympathetic than disappointed that I did not have her as a witness. Even with the little time we had to spend with her—every other weekend at her place as kids—she was always supportive.

That is her greatest parenting strength, her supportiveness. Given the logistics after the divorce, Dad was bound to be more influential in terms of our development. No one, however, has been more supportive of me than my mom. I could write what I thought was a garbage paper in school, and she would say, "I really liked it." I could shoot what I thought was a terrible score in a golf tournament, and she would remind me, "Many of us wouldn't be able to shoot that score." Although, many times she could; she was a strong golfer herself. As a matter of fact, she introduced me to the sport. And when I struggled with the learning process, she would say, "It's okay. We're just out here to have fun."

I thought she was just being a mom, saying nice things because that's what moms do, but she truly believes in us. Her support and her love for us is unconditional, and that foundation, whether from a distance or not, goes a long way to carry someone through difficult times.

I think Mom has a lot of that old Cyndi Lauper track in her blood, but I know her life is much richer than one song. I think if asked in a serious setting to answer that question again, there would be a different, more nuanced answer. I believe sometimes she is afraid to open up too much for fear of being hurt, either by past traumas that would resurface or the judgements of those she opened up to. And the reason I believe that is because I often share the same fear.

I think my mom wants to have fun, but I don't think she *just* wants to have fun. I think she wants more than that too. I know we've had a complicated mother-son relationship, but I'm proud of how far we've come and the way we've worked to make it stronger by looking forward and not backward. I hope to be as supportive to her as she's been for me, whatever it is she may want in this life.

THE LAKE HOUSE

THE LAKE HOUSE isn't real, at least not yet. Perhaps it is only meant to be a metaphor, a long and glorious victory lap, a coronation of sorts, a grand gift for a job well done. You could call it the Holy Grail, perhaps a lifetime achievement award. It's symbolic of that thing you want after the bulk of your heavy lifting for one lifetime is done. For my dad, it's the ability to have his morning coffee while watching the sun rise over the lake. And then catch a few walleyes before the sun sets.

My dad is a fucking warrior, in part because he has to be, but also because he didn't want us to have to be. He would climb Mount Everest in a blizzard if it's spared us an ounce of suffering. He spent most of his childhood dirt poor on a farm eating far too many cheese sandwiches. To this day he can barely touch a slice of cheddar with his bare fingers. When things were good, he was up early doing farm labor. When he got in trouble, he was up even earlier shoveling shit. Grandpa was not always Pastor B.

I was fortunate to experience the softer side of Grandpa, the one tenderized by grandchildren and Disney movies. Dad was raised by a firmer, hard-driving authority figure. The times were different, and so was their situation. Intimidation and fear were popular motivational factors in those times. Financial stress does not leave much time for relaxation either. You learn how to work your ass off for something, or you have nothing. Dad wanted more for us. He wanted us to be safe and comfortable and know we were loved. For thirty-eight years of my life, I have never ended a day or a conversation with my dad without each of us saying "I love you" to the other.

When my mom moved away, he learned how to raise two young boys on his own. When he eventually found his future second wife, he learned how to raise a stepdaughter, Ashley, whom he would soon adopt. He essentially raised another half generation of children, my younger brother Tyler and my youngest sister Nikki, who is eighteen years younger than I am. My best friend in high school once referred to him as a "genetic jackhammer."

I should note I adjusted better to my added siblings on Dad's side. I was older, and our familial arrangement was clearly permanent at that time. Although Ashley's penchant for running around nude at age two or three when we first met her did take a little getting used to. She also cried during every cartoon she ever watched and even when the batteries for the remote control died. Nikki was a poster-child youngest who ran the house and was shockingly impervious to Dad's aura of alpha intimidation, making for a few intolerable tantrums when I visited from college and shortly thereafter. Somehow, though, she could flip the switch at any moment and become the most charming little girl you'd ever meet. Tyler was and still is a quiet, loveable teddy bear.

Ashley has since grown into a fine young mother with a litter of girls who also tend to eschew clothing. Nikki grew up as well, maintaining her charm and losing her tantrums. Tyler is now a young father himself, and Dad is loving his role as granddad. Likewise, I'm certain he loved every bit of his fatherhood, but he's had very few breaks.

After working his first job at a grain elevator, he went after his dream of being a cop. He had other job offers along the way, but he refused them all because he was convinced of his path. Eventually, he landed a job with the sheriff's department in northwest Iowa just as I was learning to walk.

As he worked himself up to chief deputy within the department, he assumed what I think was his most fulfilling work as their undercover investigator. His primary duty was to track down, infiltrate, and arrest illegal drug operations in our county. He's always been an adrenaline junkie of sorts, and working a sting operation with armed drug traffickers has to rank high on the list of adrenaline-pumping careers. Nevertheless, I rarely remember him missing a basketball game, a football game, or a band concert of ours.

When the time was right, he assumed the duties of sheriff. He always told us he didn't like the attention or the politics, but I do think there was something about the job, the leadership aspect of being in charge, that he took to more than he let on.

As his son, I had the opportunity to meet most of the people who worked for him, and I could tell they looked up to him in almost the same way I did. I'm sure he demanded a lot of them, but I have no doubt he supported them and inspired them by way of example.

I remember Dad detailing one of their cases that took place while he was working with the investigator who later took over his position as detective. After describing the plan and illustrating how he wanted the investigator to operate, the man looked at my dad and said, "How do you expect me to do that? We don't all have balls of steel like Blythe fucking Bloemendaal!" I know the guy who said it. I have played golf with him. I have fished with him. And I have spent time in his home. I can one hundred percent picture him saying those exact words.

I had always wondered how long my dad could operate with balls of steel. Surely all of us have to slow down at some point, don't we? Even the strongest among us can only carry the weight of the world for so long.

Around the time my dad became sheriff, my stepmom, Trish,

who worked as a licensed nurse for a number of years, started having severe headaches. She was eventually diagnosed with Chiari malformation, a narrowing of the brain stem that squeezes the tissues. She worked through it for a while, and after many tests and a couple of surgeries, she eventually quit working and went on disability. The loss of her income and the addition of the medical bills put more pressure on Dad for financial stability.

As soon as he was able, at age fifty-three, Dad retired as sheriff in order to pull retirement while simultaneously earning income at a new job. He started working a night shift at a machining company because it paid well. His typical work week is now a grueling series of four twelve-hour shifts, Monday through Thursday, from 7:00 p.m. to 7:00 a.m. Retirement is typically seen as a vacation, yet he works harder than ever, even as he continues to get older. A couple of years into his new world, we could tell he was becoming exhausted.

I always remembered my dad as someone who could stare down fear, look it square in the eye and laugh in its face. He could grimace through pain and push through to the other side. No matter what he was up against, he persevered with a cocky-ass grin, just to let you know he was thoroughly enjoying kicking life's ass.

There is a fine line between cockiness and confidence, and I think a lot of it comes down to the likeability and the humble-ness of the person. I may be biased, of course, but I saw my dad as confident. You root for cocky bastards to fall back to earth and be humbled. When wonderful, confident people start to lose their swagger to exhaustion, however, your reaction is much different. You start to miss their fire.

When a family revolves around a strong, charismatic leader, such as ours does around my dad, for better or worse, the family goes as he goes. His intensity and excitement are infectious, and when this is missing, we all feel it and miss its presence.

I asked him a number of times why he didn't just quit that

soul-sucking, sleep-depriving job and pull his second retirement, or maybe still work a retirement job but something less grueling, something during the daylight hours. He always had two responses. First, he had to get his last child through college. Second, he wanted to earn enough money to buy a lake house. For probably the first time, at least to my memory, he told me about the parts of his childhood living in Michigan, the Northwoods, near the lake. When he had finished his duties, he would tell me, he just wanted to have his morning coffee on the deck watching the sunrise.

If I'd had the money to buy the house on the spot, I would have. I missed being able to connect with Dad when he worked more normal hours, and I missed the less-drained version of his personality. I lamented the fact we couldn't have frequent phone conversations because he simply wasn't awake when everyone else was awake. And when we did talk, I missed the infectious charm he had when he was in his element and kicking life's ass. And now, as I thought about his lake house dreams, I realized I simply missed fishing with my dad.

Dad had sold his last boat shortly before I went to college. The last time we went fishing together, or really any of us went fishing at all, was the one trip we took to Canada when I was in college. When I think about Dad at his best, when his swagger is at its most infectious and exciting, it is when he is on the water hunting for fish. I thought the best chance at bringing back the spark was to get him on the water.

We were two boatless fishermen working jobs that took more from us than they gave and spending too little time connecting with each other and with our favorite shared activity. The reflections led me back to my childhood, how he raised us, and memories again of our best moments on the water. I thought about how hard he had worked and all he had been through. I wanted more for him. I felt like maybe I could climb mount Everest in a blizzard if it meant he could have more.

WHO'S THE CAPTAIN?

IT HAD BEEN BUBBLING up inside all of us separately. Dad, Brando, and I sent each other telepathic signals first and then worked our way up to a text conversation. It had been way too long since we had gone fishing. Real fishing. We needed to get a boat out on the Missouri River again. We asked our uncle and cousin to come along and bring their boat. Since we didn't have one anymore, we borrowed one from Uncle Brian (Teddy). It was a small, clunky old Sylvan, but it got us on the water. Since it'd been a while, we decided to go back to Chamberlain on Lake Francis Case to get our feet wet rather than driving further and tackling bigger water.

We certainly didn't knock 'em dead, and talking to the locals, it seemed like it might've been a bit of a down year with some spotty fishing anyway. Much to Dad's dismay, crow's foot was nowhere to be found, perhaps swallowed up by the lake after all that time. Two tits had either withered away like an aged mother after raising too many breast-fed children or lost itself among the ever-growing foliage.

Mother Nature's message was clear: Times change my sons. It's time for you to be reborn and forge new paths. And stop looking at my tits; you're both goddamn adults now, for heaven's sake!

After the trip was over, thanks to the consideration Brando gave to my extra four inches of frame, I was riding shotgun in Dad's Ford pickup as I often did. I could tell Dad and I were having another mind-meld moment. Eventually, I turned and looked at him with a bit of a smirk and said, "You know what we have to do now, right?" He smiled in acknowledgment, and we began to discuss what we wanted for a boat. I told him I'd go halfsies.

It was fun to watch the gears turning in my dad's head again. He started reminiscing about old boats he'd had—the blue Lund Cherokee and an older one he basically rebuilt himself—and talking about the boat he always wanted, a Lund Tyee. Then we started thinking about future trips to Lake Oahe and getting ourselves overly excited about the prospects of returning to Dad's old stomping grounds. It was hard to believe it had been over a dozen years.

During Thanksgiving weekend later in the fall of 2014, we went to the boat dealership where Dad got his very first boat. He remembered the man who sold it to him, a fella by the name of Mike. Years ago, when Dad had explained to Mike what he was looking for and what budget he was working with, Mike hadn't had anything on site that fit the specs, but he'd said, "I might know somebody who has something you're looking for, if you're willing to go for a ride."

They drove together to one of Mike's buddy's places to check out a boat in the man's garage. Evidently it was good enough for Dad, and I assume Mike somehow brokered the deal.

"How crazy would it be if thirty years later Mike were still selling boats here?" Dad postulated. As soon as we walked in the front door, the thirty-years-later version of Mike greeted Dad first as a new customer and then as a repeat as his mind began to put the pieces together. This was all Dad's show, which was fine by me because I knew diddley shit about buying a boat. No, I wasn't a kid anymore, but I suppose I was electively placing myself in the position of apprentice this time.

As we looked around the showroom, it became clear our decision was going to be between a Crossover, a bit of a mixture between a fishing and a pleasure-type boat, and what Dad had always wanted, the Tyee. Having asked all the questions we needed to, we left the dealership and headed to a Chinese restaurant to talk over our decision. Or maybe get an answer from a fortune cookie.

My younger brother Tyler was along with us, always a bit of a quiet, stoic fellow and even less knowledgeable about buying boats than I. He listened while we discussed pros and cons of the different boats. We were leaning toward the Crossover. It was more affordable and still had the tools we needed, so we posed the question to Tyler. When he concurred, and Dad and I had ironed out the numbers, we decided Dad would return to the store the following week to purchase the boat while I was back at home doing investment stuff.

Our timing was perfect. The dealership still had a few 2014 models left, and since the 2015 had just come out, we were likely to get a pretty good discount on the older model. The one we favored most was black and silver, and I thought it looked pretty sharp. It was the last one they had, and it seem to be a good fit.

On Dad's first night back to work at his machining job, he started fish talk with one of his coworkers by the name of . . . I'll just call him "Richard." Evidently this guy was also looking for a boat. Dad mentioned their discussion to me over the phone the next day and said he had a bit of a reputation as a weasel. I think we both started to get the sense this guy might buy the boat out from under us. Surely, we were just being paranoid.

The week passed, and the time came for Dad to head back up to the dealership and make it official. As he pulled into the parking lot, he saw his coworker "Richard" pulling out. Perhaps he was just looking? Dad walked through the door, and as Mike saw Dad's face his response was "Oh boy, you weren't coming to buy that Crossover, were you? Because that guy that just left took it."

Karma is a funny thing, though. Because of the relationship Mike and Dad had, and the fact that someone else minutes earlier had purchased what we were looking for, he decided to give us a brand new 2015 model for the same price as a 2014. And so it was. My dad and I were boat owners—he again, and I for the first time. It was the worst financial investment of my life, yet, at the same time, the best money I ever spent.

It was hard waiting until spring to use the thing, but finally in May I made a trip up to Dad's place, and we decided to head over to Spirit Lake, one of the Great Lakes of Iowa, to test the boat out for the first time and hopefully catch a few in the process.

After arriving at the ramp, we start prepping the boat for lunch. I have this nagging feeling I should be doing more, that I should be taking charge more as a grown-up, but I still didn't know what the hell to do. I was just waiting for instructions from Dad. At this point, it was still his show exclusively until he brought me into it.

Step-by-step we walk through things, and then he starts backing it into the water. This particular boat trailer had a set of rollers as opposed to the bunk setup. It's supposed to be for ease of launch, so once the boat starts floating or is on somewhat of an incline, it should fly right back off the trailer without much effort. After we got ours in the water and had the engine fired up, we still couldn't get it to release from the trailer. We had missed something.

Dad tells me to pull the boat back out of the water. I scoot it up just enough to get on dry land and get a bit past the steep incline of the ramp. We walk around to the back of the boat and realize the problem: tiedown straps. There are two straps in the back fastening the hull of the boat to the trailer to prevent it from coming off. They have to be released before the boat can release. Again, I didn't know diddly shit from anything, and Dad had never owned a trailer with straps. No big deal, easy fix.

In the process of attempting to launch the boat, we had unhooked the chain and the winch strap from the front of the trailer while it was in the water. Dad had told me to pull the boat out of the water, so I had done exactly that. One of his fatal flaws is making assumptions of people. My fatal flaw was trusting he knew exactly what we needed to do and was going to tell me word for word. Neither one of us hooked the boat back up at the front of the trailer.

Still standing at the back of the boat, we each decide to unhook a strap from either side. I heard his pop first, then I unhooked mine, and the boat started flying backward straight at me. For some crazy, unknown fucking reason, my first instinct was to catch the boat instead of getting the hell out of the way.

After the boat's initial lunge in our direction, it stopped. Did we actually catch it? Were we holding it on? Dad yells at me, "You got it?!"

"I think so," I grunted, leaning forward into the boat with all my weight.

Like The Flash he runs around to the front and latches the boat. "We're hooked," he yells. And then I let go.

So many thoughts were running through my mind at that point. Was it actually our efforts that stopped it from coming off the trailer? The initial part of the roller bed is steep to get the boat to start moving but then flattens out toward the back end. It's quite possible, since we were on fairly flat ground, that the boat simply stopped itself when it reached the back end of the rollers.

Had we still been on the incline of the ramp, I honestly don't know if our efforts would've held anything. And I also don't know if I would've actually moved out of the way or continued to try to catch the boat. It's entirely possible that over one thousand pounds of aluminum would've pulverized me before I ever got a chance to use it. When people ask me if I've ever had any near-death experiences, this is the only one I can think of. Often times I don't tell the story out of sheer embarrassment.

Dad lit a smoke. I stood staring at the boat, more than a little traumatized, part of me still worried it was somehow going to fall off yet. At this point I had zero confidence in what we were doing, and it was hard to stop shaking.

"Why didn't you latch the boat?" Dad asked. My answer was sorely lacking yet honest.

"You didn't tell me too."

"Fair enough," he said. "I suppose I make those assumptions that people know what they're doing, huh? How 'bout we keep this one to ourselves and go fish?"

We did keep it between us for a number of years, but now I'm writing it down in a book. We'll see how he feels about that later.

The water at Spirit Lake was brutally clear, and the fishing was terrible. We decided to trailer over to neighboring Silver Lake to see if we would have better luck. This time we remembered the straps.

After safely launching, Dad commented that normally there is a marker buoy indicating a rock pile off the dock. Being early spring, apparently no one had bothered to place it yet. Nevertheless, we navigated away from the dock and began to fish some old spots he remembered from years ago.

The fishing was slow, but we caught a few. And then we decided we'd had enough for the day and went to load our wannabe deathtrap feeling more than a little lucky to be vertical. As Dad got closer to the dock and I started toward the bow to tie us up, we heard a crash and a loud scraping noise. The bottom of our brand new Four-Stroke 150 Mercury found that rock pile. It was almost like suffering two flat tires on the same road trip.

After loading the boat, we saw a pretty good chunk knocked out of the tail fin, but thankfully it didn't seem to expose its guts, and no oil was leaking. The hull of the boat was fine, as only the motor fin clipped the rock. Dad would monitor the situation over the next few weeks before our subsequent trip, and it appeared no fatal damage had been done. Still, we had a comedy of errors to learn from in our first joint boat-ownership experience.

Though never quite as traumatic as nearly dry-docking and crushing our dumb asses, we had more than a few awkward experiences the first couple of years with our toy. Most of them came down to a failure to establish roles and responsibilities.

Neither of us having owned a boat since I was back in high school, I think we just started where we left off, Dad taking the kids fishing. Perhaps that time gap stunted my growth and our transition. Besides, running a boat isn't nearly as common a rite of passage as, say, driving a car. No one *needs* to learn to operate a boat. But now I owned half of one and wanted to learn, yet I felt a little awkward asking Dad to teach me, almost as if we should have done this long ago and the window of teaching opportunity had passed. Pride gets in the way as an adult sometimes, and teaching becomes more awkward.

Then I got over myself. I told him on future trips I wanted to run the boat and have him take the mentor role. Perfect. Decision made. With one problem behind us, we stumbled into the next two: communicating in the mentoring process and actually committing to it.

Had I been fishing alone, I would have taught myself in the same way I learn anything else, by trial and error. I would've pulled up to a spot, fished it, and seen what happened. If nothing, move on. Just keep learning. But being in the boat with my dad, an experienced fish finder in years past, I felt more pressure to pick the "right spot."

I would cruise along shoreline structure trying to read Dad's mind as he scanned everything, then randomly ask, "What about this spot?"

"I don't know. What do you think?"

Then I would pull into that spot and ease off the throttle and
Dad might say, "Do you really wanna fish around all these boats?"

"I don't know. I guess it crossed my mind."

"Keep going," he'd say.

"Here?"

"No, keep going. If we're going to move, let's really move."
Whatever the hell that means. I guess it wasn't moving until we
moved at least a mile? Two miles? Did he just want a different
spot or was he looking for an entirely different piece of the lake?
Was he looking for different water temperature? Clarity? Just to
get away from boats? A piece of structure which better caught
his eye? Or did he even really know?

It became clear to me things were different now. Dad didn't
have his badass Jean-Claude Van Damme hair anymore, and I
was no longer a wide-eyed kid who saw him as an all-knowing
mythical figure. He was human, not Hercules, and at this point
we were just two guys trying to figure it out, neither of us taking
charge nor fully relinquishing it either.

On another trip we were fishing the river below the dam by
Pierre, technically Lake Sharpe, but only a few miles from the
spillway and more river-like. After launching at the marina, there
was some skinny water to navigate, some of it fairly shallow. I
was doing my best to follow my electronics and my contour map
on the screen. Dad was more programmed toward eyeballing
shorelines and following other boats he assumed to be locals.

As the river made a bend, eventually I needed to swing out
wide to avoid a shallow mud bar. Based on my map, I still had a
few hundred yards to go. Dad's senses told him I needed to turn
sooner. In the heat of the moment, my child-like, listen-to-dad
persona punched my logical adult consciousness in the gut and
took over the steering wheel. I turned too early, and our boat
wound up beached in the mud under about a foot of water.

Later during the same trip, back up on the big water above
the dam, we put in at a marina right next to a bend in the lake.

As I throttled up to get out to the main lake, Dad says, "Get across the lake to the other side."

"What other side?" I asked?

"Just cross."

For me, there were a bunch of different ways to "cross" at this point. I could cross going south, I could cross going west, and I could cross going north or any which way in between. There would be a difference of perhaps six to eight miles from any of these final destinations. Did Dad simply mean cross straight ahead the way the boat was pointed? He didn't say as much. We must've argued about this for a full minute or two before I just throttled up and drove.

Even when we got back home from this trip, we had a hard time letting it go. As the family was sitting out on the porch, Dad comes outside from the house with a pen and paper in hand. He sits down at the patio table and starts drawing a crude map of the lake with an arrow stretching "across" it.

"This is across, is it not?"

Brandon and Tyler shake their heads. Normally the quiet one, Tyler quips, "Would you guys just quit this already?"

I did a lot of reflection after some of these trips. I thought a lot about communication styles and the way people learn. Brandon and I talked about some of these events a number of times. And eventually I did talk to Dad about it as well. We've gotten much better since then.

Dad's big admission was that he makes too many assumptions. He has since done a better job of filling in some of those gaps, often catching himself in the act. I think he also understands how differently I visualize things and choose my words, but I'm not sure he quite comprehends them or knows what to do with them yet.

I think my dad's teaching methods also tend to lead with the intention of protection rather than educating. I know full well his own learning process was rough with Grandpa. As a result, I think Dad went too far the other direction when raising us.

I can't think of many things he did wrong as a dad, but one of them was probably not letting us fall often enough or not pushing us to do some of the things we didn't find pleasurable as children. Though we never lived on a farm, he didn't have me do the equivalent of any shit shoveling in my childhood, and perhaps I needed a little bit of that.

When he teaches now, it's very literal and direct. It's as if he is reading aloud from an internal instruction manual: "Turn left, throttle up a bit, not too fast! NO! DON'T HIT THAT WAVE LIKE THAT!"

Sometimes I want to yell at him "JUST LET ME FUCK IT UP ONCE!" I reflexively let myself get sucked into the tunnel vision of simply following directions. I'm not learning how to feel it. I'm not gaining any intuition. And I won't be able to do it next time when he's not telling me word by word.

These were hard things to work through, but we got there.

A few years later, we were making our second trip of the year to Devils Lake, North Dakota. It was a windy day in early fall, and we knew the lake was going to get rough as it often does. Still, given the forecasted winds of twenty-five miles per hour, we figured we could handle getting across the lake. We started on the calm side, but when it didn't produce, we boogied across.

We tucked up into a semiprotected bay and anchored on a rock pile to do some vertical jigging. We got a few decent walleyes and stuck it out for a couple hours. It was rough enough, but we were protected from the full-on waves of the main lake.

In the midafternoon the skies started to gray a little more. And then the temperature started to drop. And then we saw some clouds pushing in which had an angry front to them. Within minutes, the wind kicked up another ten miles per hour. We still had to get to the other shoreline to load the boat. We came to the conclusion we had better get our asses moving before it was too late.

For our last few trips, I had been exclusively running the

boat. As I pulled out of the bay and around the corner, however, I must admit, for a half second, my old instincts damn near turned the wheel back over. My internal argument happened quite fast, as it had to in such a situation, and this time it was my adult conscience who pushed little Brett aside and said "I got this."

I have never seen waves like that before, consistently six to seven feet, occasionally closer to eight. When our boat would go down into the trough, we couldn't see above the next peak. There wasn't much to think about, however. I had a straight line from me to the boat ramp. I simply had to keep that bow pointed into the waves for three miles until I got there.

I had never received such a beating from water. Each wave we encountered created a bone-crushing slap, reverberating through the whole of the boat and into our bones right up through the skull. After ten minutes of this, my head was pounding. My legs felt strong but were slowly tiring.

I learned from my dad to drive the boat in rough water while standing, almost like riding a Jet Ski. For me it helped to look above the windshield when it was getting soaked with waves, and it felt easier to absorb the pounding with my legs than to sit on a pedestal seat putting the brunt of the blow into my back.

As we continued on, we were both standing. We should've been wearing lifejackets. I didn't know exactly how big the waves were going to be when we originally pulled out of the bay, and there was no way we could take our eyes off the waves now to start fucking around in the storage compartments. In fact, as we hit one particularly nasty wave, Dad actually fell down onto the floor of the boat.

"You okay?" I said without taking my eyes off the water.

"Yep. I'm fine. You're good."

Sure, I was afraid, but it was also a bit of an adrenaline rush. It felt like one of those "own-your-shit" moments. I channeled the best of my father, but I also did it my way. He never said a word. As we got halfway across the lake, feeling more comfortable with the situation we were in, I casually asked him, "You wanna stop and fish the towers for a while since we're here?"

"Ha! Yeah, sure thing."

Normally a ten-minute boat ride or less, it took us an hour and fifteen minutes to reach the landing. We had intended to fish the other shore once we got there, but I drove straight to the ramp. My head and my neck were done, probably the first time I ever initiated the end of a fishing day.

If my dad was ever nervous, he didn't say so. As we were eating dinner in the restaurant that night, he told me of a time he and Grandpa had been out on the water when things got rough.

"Dad was up in the bow freaking out. He was yelling at me how we weren't gonna make it, it's too rough. I stopped the boat and said, 'Dad, listen to me. This is my thing now. We're gonna get to the other side. Just sit there, shut up, and hold on tight, alright? I got this. Just trust me.' He spun right around and sat there dead straight. His hands were purple and blue choking that seat, bobbing up and down the whole way. But we made it."

Dad squeezed out a wry smile. I got a shiver up my neck. He took a sip of water, then continued.

"You did a great job out there. You reminded me of myself when I was your age."

What I heard was "You're the captain now."

A RECOVERING HEALTH ADDICT

A COWORKER and friend of mine tells me I look like an air traffic controller. I have a pair of wraparound blue-blocking glasses, the ones with the amber tint you could use to shield your eyes while welding. I have a pair of over-the-ear noise-canceling headphones to help me focus and block out the annoyances of folks sniffing, coughing, chewing, tapping hands, clicking on keyboards, basically any repetitious noise pollution.

For added protection, I also have blue-blocking screens taped over my computer monitors. I have a wristband connected to a cord and plugged into the grounding plug on my electrical outlet to reduce the effects of ambient electromagnetic waves around me. My shoes are off, and I'm standing on an acupuncture mat to improve the blood flow in my legs.

I have a stack of supplements sitting on my desk I take on a schedule throughout the workday. I have three fifty-ounce bottles of pure reverse-osmosis filtered water, pH balanced for body alkalization. I take breaks every thirty minutes to move about the office and do regular stretches and exercises at my desk while working.

∿

I felt self-conscious about it all initially, so I introduced it slowly, one item at a time. Soon my coworkers just sort of got used to it, I think. If my work had to be done at this desk through this computer, I was going to do everything I could to not let my body turn into a miserable, uncomfortable, painful pile of piss. And I think some of it even kinda, sorta worked.

When the weather was nice outside, I used to take walks around the nature path we had out behind the office building. When I got far enough from the windows where I didn't think anyone else would notice, I used to take off my shoes and socks and walk barefoot in the grass. This act was still a bit eccentric, but it was perhaps more "normal" than some of my other strategies.

One particular day, I must not have been far enough away from the windows. Someone had called security, and they came out to check on the barefoot wanderer outside. Standing there in the grass, holding my shoes, I saw an officer in uniform approaching me.

"How are you today, sir?" they said, nearing my position.

"Good. Just taking a walk. How are you?"

"Good. We had a report of someone walking barefoot that the employees thought may be suspicious. Can I see your badge please?"

"Sure."

"Fair enough. So, you *are* an employee. I might just recommend you wear your shoes from now on?"

"Understood."

If you are thinking I am at all embellishing this story, either the security guard encounter or the other gadgets and quirks, I can assure you I am not. In fact, I left out a few things so far. There was the pulsed electromagnetic pocket machine I ran on my lower back for most of the day, clipped to my belt buckle. It was supposed to accelerate your body's ability to heal, and the worst of my pain was my lower back. I got a good deal at $1,400.

I also spent about $400 on a device to beam infrared healing light into my brain through my nasal cavity. This was mostly a nighttime activity, however, as infrared light is best used in the evening to stimulate melatonin production and sleep for recovery.

I had been fitted for a special set of reading glasses to help eyestrain, headaches, and eventually neck soreness. I had tons of different home massage devices, foam rollers, heating pads, pain creams, magnesium salts, and on and on and on. I basically spent my entire day trying to either prevent, reduce, or fix various pains and discomfort I incurred as a tax during my career.

Prior to all the gadgets, I had completely changed my diet. These days it's pretty straightforward: I essentially avoid wheat and dairy and excess sugar whilst trying to eat a lot of vegetables and healthy fats and proteins. But the process of going through all the elimination diets and learning how to read labels and figure out the new, healthier foods I might still enjoy eating was massively exhausting albeit not entirely unrewarding. My ego feels like it deserves an honorary degree in nutrition at this point.

I also researched and experimented heavily in as many different exercise programs as I did nutrition programs. They would range anywhere from extremely intense CrossFit-style exercises to complete low- or no-contact tai chi and yoga-style practices. Again, to some extent it was worth the time and effort, as there were some things I kept as part of my ongoing lifestyle habits, but the process was a bit of self-inflicted brutality, especially on top of eight to ten hours of my "real job."

When you add it all up, I was trying desperately to live a happy life with less pain, but it consumed my entire day to the point where there was not even a minute to spare for the actual living part. Still, it's hard to see the big picture for yourself. Even if part of you suspects these efforts are not working, the ego refuses to let go of something it worked so hard to learn, build, or purchase.

If I admit I'm wrong, I also have to admit I wasted all that money, too. I can't tell you exactly how much I spent on what I suppose you would loosely consider to be "healthcare," but if you exclude actual doctor bills, include all of the above, and then throw in the physical therapy, chiropractic, acupuncture, and massage therapy, there's a chance I was pushing the $100,000 mark after roughly five years of this circus.

My mom and I have a fair amount in common, not the least of which is roughly fifty percent of her genetic code. She has long been focused on health and wellness herself. Before the divorce, she started a business out of our house called Health & Diet. Later Dad helped her find an office location in town. Her mission was to help other women like her to eat well and exercise. She was a collector of Jane Fonda-like workout tapes and food recipes, not too unlike the content I began digging into when I reached adulthood.

As she got older, she struggled more with her abdominal region too, digestive issues like mine but also scar tissue and the resulting abdominal pain. At over nine pounds, I wasn't a small baby, and I chose to attempt entering the world upside down, prompting her doctor to recommend a cesarian section. Or was I right-side up? Whichever way is the wrong way. She tried a natural birth again with my brother, but it didn't work. I can imagine four kids and four C-sections put a lot of stress on her body.

The more we talked about our own health struggles, the more we realized we shared a lot of them. She began to feel frustratingly inhibited in her active lifestyle of tennis, golf, and general exercise and would sometimes exclaim, "I just wanna frickin' do the things I wanna do! It sucks, Brett!"

Beyond the digestive issues, we both struggled with fatigue and chronic pain as well as anxiety. I always knew her to be a nervous type who had a hard time sitting still. I used to give her a hard time about that and insist she just relax and sit with us.

As my own adult life became busy and stressful, I came to understand how she felt. I could relax under normal daily situations, but put under pressure, it all changed. I had to do something, fix something, and keep on the move. At its worst, I had to exit the situation. Mom must have more stress within her than I originally knew.

I have always been uber protective of her, even from a young age. I remember sitting on the beach once while Dad was pulling her in the tube behind his fishing boat. My Aunt Bobbi commented on all the exhaust coming off the motor and how it appeared to be swamping my mom's face. Bobbi was laughing, perhaps mildly concerned about discomfort. I started panicking and asking if we needed to "save her."

When Mom got married to Bruce, his groomsmen carried out some kind of wedding reception ritual. They "abducted" Mom as one of them hoisted her up on his shoulder, and they took her out for a drink at the bar. Mom was laughing, a clear sign that everything was okay, but I became hysterical. My instincts told me they were going to hurt her, and eventually my dad and uncle had to come pick me and my brother up and take us home.

Once I was all grown up and "smart," I thought for sure I could save her from her pain and fix her medical problems if she adopted my newfound methods. By then I realized not everything I did was necessary or even helpful. But I thought I was boiling some of it down to the most beneficial strategies which might actually be worth the time and money to continue. I began sending her research articles to read, diet plans to try, and exercises to perform.

After a few months of this, I began to feel uneasy about what I was doing. This educational process started to feel similar to the way Dad and I had approached boat school, which gave me pause. The more I evaluated it, the more I saw other aspects I could address differently.

At least initially, I wasn't helping someone who asked, I was offering unsolicited advice. Furthermore, though I didn't view it this way at the time, I was trying to "fix" her, though I now understand no one is inherently broken. And I wasn't giving her the tools to help her understand, I was giving her an instruction manual, trying to teach her the way Dad had tried teaching me with the boat.

Moreover, I was doing it to spare her from pain when pain might be part of the lesson. Dad had been doing his best with what he knew, but now I knew better and had to do better. He hadn't made me shovel shit as a kid, but maybe Mom needed to do her own digging at this time in her life. Not that I didn't care, but there is value in finding your own way. Moreover, my role was never meant to be instructive but rather supportive.

From that point forward, I let Mom dig. I would help if she asked, but it wasn't my place to fix anyone else. Even the idea that I could strikes me as a bit absurd now in hindsight.

It was difficult to watch my mom traverse the same paths I did and fight my old urges to interject my knowledge. It was almost as if she was on a parallel timeline just a few years behind me. If I was unable to notice how much I was flailing in the mirror when I was at that stage, it all became much clearer watching my mom because I recognized her situation as my own. And that's when I realized I might not know as much as I thought I did, and that I might have gone too far with my health crusades.

Now that she was armed with a smart phone and some web-surfing savvy, she became her own research crusader as well. Just as I was turning a corner and realizing that obsessively overana-lyzing one's health can actually be detrimental to it, I saw Mom toiling in the same quicksand from which I was trying to escape. And I was partly responsible for convincing her to jump in with me.

Mom began flooding my inbox with article after article she thought might be causing one problem or another. Knowing that I had been doing extensive research on my own health, she came to see me as some sort of subject-matter expert. She wanted me to double check her work, almost as if I were her surrogate doctor.

As time went on, the information started coming in at an exponentially faster pace. Not only could I not keep up with it while trying to tend to my own ills and a full-time job, it started to seem as though she was digging for the sake of digging. There wasn't an end game. And as she described it, most or none of what she was doing was helping, at least not to her satisfaction, so she kept digging more and more frantically until it seemed as though the digging was the actual source of distress. Or, at the very least, a distraction from the truth of what really needed addressing.

I was always keen on finding the root cause, digging deeper and deeper not to bandage symptoms but to fix the problem at its source. From a logical, analytical perspective, this is quite smart. I wasn't going to take Advil to block the pain, I was going to fix the problem so I wouldn't have pain. It wasn't until watching my mom play out what I had just been through that I had an epiphany.

Pain literally is a creation of the mind. It's a warning signal developed to keep us safe. If you touch a hot stove, your finger burns, you pull your finger away, and you (hopefully) don't do it again. My pain and discomfort had lasted for years. Every single day I had dealt with back pain, neck pain, muscle stiffness and soreness, weakness, growing inflexibility, and dropping energy levels. I was sitting on top of the hot stove for eight or ten hours a day while researching and trying to understand my pain. I never noticed what my body was trying to tell me until I saw it with my mom.

These warning systems our bodies have are a gift. They are something to be treasured and listened to, not annoyances to be shut up. I had been spending years of time and money on external "things" I thought were root-cause solutions but were actually just more and more expensive ways of masking or dulling my warning systems. I suppose I deserve some kudos for not abusing drugs or alcohol and attempting to find "healthy" fixes, yet I was still misguided as to what I was actually trying to solve.

My answers were not out there, they were in here (I'm pointing to my chest now). Finally, I decided to dig deeper on the inside. Instead of shutting up the pain, I sat quietly and listened. There are a lot of things we intuitively know if we just take the time to pay attention. It's simple, but it's not easy. Much like the work I was doing before with all the research, I would have to do a similar type of internal work to unravel what was going on inside this time.

I spent my money more wisely on things like therapy. I spent my time more wisely on things like meditation and journaling. I was trying to go deeper. Even the act of writing this book is part of that process. I went through my relationships: with my mom, with my dad, and with previous significant others. I went through my needs and my wants as a person, trying to reconnect with my inner self and my inner child, removing the context of my current career and financial needs.

You feel as though you're tearing yourself up, and maybe you are. Perhaps it's necessary to find yourself—or perhaps more accurately remember and uncover—and rebuild as needed.

One of the best ways to connect with the inner self is by reconnecting with nature. And one of the best gateways I know of to connect with nature is, for me, through fishing. I started to spend a lot more time on the water. The more I was out there, the more it all started to come back to me. Things felt simple again, and I remembered what life was like when I was living it for myself instead of for others or external goals. What I didn't know yet was whether this was just an escape or actually a solution.

There is a beauty to this process, however. Whether you like it or not, it brings forth real answers through truth. The analytical mind, something very stubborn within me, loves to sit and spin and find other answers, ways around these inevitable truths.

Those answers are never satisfying. They never feel right. The only time I feel as though I'm making progress is when I address the hard stuff that comes out of my intuition. It's not fun, but it is rewarding. It's progress, and it actually makes a difference for me and how I feel. It's living rather than escaping. Instead of flailing like a fish out of water, I dive in and deal with my true, inner world, the one where nothing but my own thoughts swim.

Again, I reached out to my mom. This time I did not have any solutions to offer, but I opened up to her about my anxiety issues and how working on my emotions helped to ease my physical ailments as well. I suspected it would help her too, but I didn't want to pretend I knew this time. Likewise, I learned the importance of finding your own path, and she deserved space to do the same. I merely wanted to be supportive and listen. Should she later decide she wants to dive in and look at everything down there, I hope she knows we will be there when she comes back up.

(MY) SOLACE

FOR THE LONGEST TIME, I hadn't even heard the complete version of one of my favorite songs. It was titled "Solace," and had a forty-five second intro on a YouTube video. For whatever reason, Myles Kennedy and Alter Bridge kept the rest to themselves for about a decade until finally including it as a bonus track on a live concert album in 2017, *Live at the O2 Arena + Rarities.*

Talk about ramping up the hype! Could you imagine a movie trailer coming out ten years before the full-length film hit theaters? There must be more to the story. Let's speculate for a moment.

It's possible they felt it wasn't one of the stronger tracks and didn't warrant making the cut for any albums, but then why give people the teaser of the intro? Maybe they liked the idea but didn't know where to go with it yet. Maybe they thought fans would make interpretations and they were looking to crowd-source the song. Maybe they knew they wanted to write a song about solace but hadn't yet worked out what solace meant for them, so it was out there as a placeholder and a reminder of what they were working toward.

If Myles was unsuccessfully looking for his solace, he wasn't alone. I waited for his lyrics same as I waited for my own meaning and the epiphany that would usher it in.

Searching for something as conceptual and subjective as solace is not at all like looking for a lost dog. You don't have a visual description of your target, and you may not recognize it the instant you see it. I personally found it difficult to ascertain the difference between solace and distraction. During a time of suffering, a good action movie might be a pleasant distraction but has no lasting affect after the credits roll and the houselights come up to illuminate reality once again.

Solace is much deeper and more enduring. It brings about strength and support to work through issues and continue living a fulfilling life. It is constant amidst change and reassuring in the way it continues to show up for you. For some, this may be faith or religion, a relationship with something bigger than the self.

For me, the something bigger is nature. The reliability of a sunrise and a sunset. The cyclical changing of the seasons. Water always flowing downhill. Always the water. And fishing is my meditation, my preferred vehicle for connecting with nature's flow.

I am most at peace on my boat, on the open water, casting a line into the endless horizon, waiting to be interrupted by a hungry fish. Meditation does not have to be sitting still in the full lotus position with your eyes closed. It's anything holding your focus in the present, keeping you immersed in the task at hand. Fishing isn't a religion, at least in the organized way, but if you do it right, it is spiritual. It's a gateway to the heavens of nature.

Fishing brought me back from the edge, helping me let go of years of self-induced suffering and remember simpler ways. It brought me back in touch with the cycles of nature and reminded me of the patience it requires to live with her in flow and harmony. You can't make fish bite, but if you put in time and pay attention, you will be provided with what you need.

If you listen, the fish will also tell you what *they* need. Bigger baits or smaller baits? Fast or slow? Hopping, dancing, swimming, or wiggling? Color? Sound? Vibration? To be successful in fishing is to be successful at meditation by being observant and paying attention. The answers come in time when you are open to them. The quiet periods in between become your test.

You can't cheat fishing; you have to play their game. Your success depends on their participation. It's not like blitzing a quarterback by overpowering an offensive line. You can't use skill alone as you might when jumping above a defender to dunk a basketball. You have to learn their ways and meet them in the middle, a compromise between human and fish. Fishing is a physical art that brings us in touch with our instincts, instincts we forget while living life on autopilot.

The more I started fishing again, the more I started to remember. I started to remember the way my body would move in response to something I've visualized in my head. I remembered what it was like to simply react, to not have time to think. If we had to think about every muscle, joint, tendon, and bone we intended to move in order to accomplish a physical task, we'd never manage anything. Certain movements can be trained, but movement itself must be intuitive at its basic level.

Fishing helped me get out of my head and into deeper parts of my being. Focusing on a singular thing left me no room for overanalyzing myself. Intellectually, I understood this concept, but it took something important and purposeful enough to be willing to shift my headspace. I wanted this; I simply had to manifest it. Instead of focusing on what I didn't want, pain and suffering, I started focusing on what I did want, to be out on the water fishing. The renewed sense of purpose gave me strength to go through everything else to get it. I had a growth vehicle again, and when we grow, we heal.

Initially, it just felt good to be back, to have the sun on my skin, the fresh air circulating through my nose, the water slowly rocking underneath my feet. The sights and sounds of the scenery and the life around me were peaceful and healing in their own right. I knew it was working when I stopped being content with merely being out there and started to regain a burning desire to improve my craft and succeed at catching fish.

The more I focused on this purpose, the less I thought about my own suffering. And the less I thought about my own suffering, the quieter the suffering became. It was almost as if by focusing on it I was feeding it, fanning the flames with oxygen. By letting go of what I didn't want and chasing what I did, it all seemed to change.

Perhaps it's time to let go.

There's another Alter Bridge song full of meaning in my life, "Watch Over You." I learned how to play it on guitar, and one of my jam partners and I have gotten lost in it at least a hundred times. It's a beautifully melodic tune in open G requiring unique yet rewarding fretwork. The open G rings so warm and pure in its resolve, like the gates of heaven opening up and welcoming you home. I played it while Dad spoke at my grandpa's gravesite the day we laid him to rest, wondering silently to myself, "Who *will* watch over him?"

I had a daydream once, born of fanboy fantasy. Myles was doing an acoustic solo tour, and one event was within driving distance of my home. They were offering VIP packages to meet him and hang out backstage for a couple hours after the show. If I told him "Watch Over You" is my favorite song to play, would he offer to have me join him? I wondered. Could I play his Taylor guitar, the one I based my own Taylor purchase on, while he sang and maybe riffed and soloed over top? Would he get half the kick out of it that I would?

Eventually, when the full version of "Solace" was released, I got to see if the lyrics lived up to the hype of the guitar inro. It starts out:

"When we drift with the tide, are we gone forever?"

"And when we find ourselves, I ask my soul."

"But it doesn't know."

I'm grateful mine now does. My fanboy wants to call up Myles and let him know the good news. Then the last prechorus:

"My faith, it grows."

"No need to question, I already know."

"I've found a way."

"To a better tomorrow, a little today."

Happy for ya, Myles. Solidarity, brother.

LUNCH BREAK

BACK IN ELEMENTARY SCHOOL, all I could think about after sitting down at a desk at 8:20 a.m. was how much time there was left until lunch. I was a ravenous child with the metabolism of a hummingbird, but I also looked for any excuse to avoid reading and writing for twenty-five glorious minutes. Ironic now, isn't it? Also, twenty-five minutes isn't nearly enough time for this guy to eat a meal. I usually sat down to my desk with chipmunk cheeks full of everything I couldn't bear to watch tumbling into a trash can.

What was my favorite school food, you might ask? Easy. Rectangle pizza. Or fish sandwiches. Or hamburgers. Or the chili with cinnamon rolls. Rib sandwich days were pretty awesome too. Oh, and they had this basket of peanut butter sandwiches at the end of the line every day, and you could take as many as you wanted, beautifully creamy peanut butter that didn't stick to the roof of your mouth. I always wondered how they pulled that off. A few years and a few thousand sandwiches later, I theorized they must put actual butter, dairy butter, on the sandwich first before the peanut variety, and I'm now realizing I've gone on far too long about peanut butter sandwiches.

By my freshman year of college, little had changed except my height, my weight, and the company. Each day we would parade through the hallway, rounding up the troops of White Hall to march into the servery—our institution's unique term for a cafeteria—and pillage the various buffet lines of all moderately-edible sustenance fifteen or twenty young adult males could slam down their gullets. First one done got PlayStation priority for Madden Football. I always lost. In between bites, you could occasionally hear words like "pass" or "tackle" or "you suck." It was higher education at its finest.

Lunch has always been sacred to me. When I was younger, if I missed it, I was afraid my metabolism would eat me from the inside out. As an adult, it was still very much biologically necessary but also a chance to connect with people and perhaps make friends, the kind who know you inside and out. Eating together breaks down barriers. If you've eaten lunch with me, we've spent a lot of time together, given my painfully slow pacing, and I probably consider you to be a wonderful human to share something that important.

When I set out into the real world, solidifying lunch plans was one of my first priorities. It was easy at my first job as a bank examiner. We worked as a crew onsite at our target bank, so we'd all leave together around noon to find a good restaurant. Once I landed a job at my first investment company, I had to work for it.

Most days around midmorning I would start recruiting fellow eaters. During the first few months, I would cast a wider net in order to meet a broader range of people and forge strategic working relationships. Later I wound up working full time on a project team for an intense software implementation and became pretty tight with that group. As it turned out, most of them also ate food.

From that point on, we had a more fixed crew, a lunch club of sorts with a standing calendar invitation. I was the lone business member, and the rest of the group was usually from IT, information technology to the layperson. Occasionally, we would invite other "guest attendees," but the core remained pretty consistent for a number of years thereafter.

One of the regulars was Alina. We had both started employment with the company around the same time, she probably three months or so after me. I remember watching her arrive for her interview because she had to walk by my desk to get to the conference room. She had an arrogant walk and a smug face that told everyone off without saying a word and seemed very unapproachable. Or perhaps my lens was merely distorted by patriarchal influence.

As I would learn, she was completely unaware of the external impression she created. She's protective of her inner world until she trusts you, and apparently it manifests in the way she carries herself. Looking back on that first impression, it's hard to believe it's even the same person. My adjusted view of her would be that she is confident yet cautious.

Two important things you should know about Alina: she loves pranks, and she hates hugs.

Perhaps my favorite all-time prank of hers was one she referred to as "Cat Facts." Another member of our lunch crew, a woman by the name of Patti, had a tendency to leave her phone unattended and unlocked, probably poor form for an IT professional, but that's not really relevant here. Besides, it was her personal phone anyway. Back to the point.

Alina went into the phone and renamed her own contact info as "Cat Facts." She then started sending messages a few hours later with banal information about cats, things like "Cats can jump up to six times their length" or "Some cats are ambidextrous, but 40% are either right- or left-pawed." Just below each fact it stated "Only $.99 per fact! Reply 'unsubscribe' to be removed from the list."

Each time Patti tried to unsubscribe, however, Alina would just send her another cat fact. This went on for a few days until Patti finally brought it up at one of our lunches, complaining how she couldn't get unsubscribed from this damn "Cat Facts" scam and was probably being charged money the whole time. We tried to maintain straight faces as long as we could before cracking. I nearly choked on my water with laughter as Alina broke the news.

Matter of fact, these pranks were a broader part of the culture at my first investment company, even before Alina arrived. About a month into starting the job, I arrived at work one day, sat down at my desk, and heard my phone ring. As I perused my desk, I realized the phone was nowhere to be seen, and the ring was a bit muted. It was coming from my drawer, and I didn't remember putting it there.

When I tried to open the drawer, it wouldn't budge because it was locked. When I looked for my key, it was nowhere to be seen either. I probably should've taken that thing home with me for the night.

Meanwhile, one cubicle row away from me, I could hear some of my friendly coworkers apparently on a conference call. I heard snippets of conversation such as "Microsoft" and "system is down" until it devolved into outright laughter, and I noticed they were watching me struggle to open my drawer and answer my phone. They even went through the work of tucking the phone cord underneath the desk into the drawer so I didn't suspect anything upon my arrival. The pranksters always took great pride in their work.

We also used to attend an event called the Golden Circle Games. Companies downtown would put together teams to compete in a variety of events such as tug-of-war, rubber chicken toss, Hula-Hoop relays—basically games that had some level of physical skill but could also be completed under the influence of alcohol.

We had a pretty strong showing the first year, specifically dominating the tug-of-war contest. After reigning victorious in our last match, I remember high-fiving a few people and then giving Alina a hug, at which point she shriveled up like a skittish cat being petted by an overly zealous toddler. And that was when I learned about her personal-space issues.

Since that time, the only successful and semiwelcomed hug I was able to coax out of her was the night of her going-away party years later. It took probably six beers, an early warning, and ten minutes of reasoning.

This was all part of what made the first few years as an investment professional such a great experience for me. It's not that we goofed around all day long and didn't get any work done, but we had a good sense of camaraderie and strong working relationships which actually led to accomplishing amazing things professionally as well. We felt like a team. We had a sense of purpose and belonging and were all more or less aligned toward the same goals, picking each other up and helping one another along the way.

Slowly and steadily, things began to change. Management shuffled, employees came and went, and the culture shifted. Pranks became few and far between, as did other after-work social events. The Golden Circle Games went out of favor. Perhaps most sadly, our lunch club started to dissipate.

Alina and I had become pretty good coworkers and friends at this point, however, and I remember wondering whether or not she would find it awkward if we continued to do the lunches, just the two of us. She must not have, because we kept it up for over ten years across two different places of employment and beyond.

On an intellectual level, she has to be one of the most fascinating people I've ever known. I absolutely despise small talk, which can often dominate workplace lunches. I typically needed a break from actual work discussion, as opposed to a so-called working lunch, and she valued the same. After over a dozen years, we still never seem to run out of interesting topics of discussion.

Life is ever-changing, so naturally we seek out a few constants in people we can trust and rely on over time, people there with you from point A to point B and then C, D, and E, who can relate to the entire arc of the plot. If my investment career were a season of *Survivor,* she would be the only coworker from the original cast who was still on my island.

She was there during the early days of our first company, when we had potentially the best professional job environment of our lives and didn't yet know how lucky we were. She was there when the sale of the company finally started to show itself and the culture started shifting to something new. She had left shortly before the company was sold again and all of our jobs were dismissed, but it wasn't long before I landed a job at her new employer, as did a few of our other coworkers since it was one of the two major local firms in our business.

She's definitely the only coworker, and one of only a few friends, to whom I can divulge almost anything. In order to get any true advice from someone, they almost have to know and understand the whole picture. After a dozen years of near daily encounters, one can connect a hell of a lot of dots.

She may also be the most introspective person I know. I always marveled at how well she could look back on things and do the processing necessary to make sense out of it and find a better way forward. I thought of myself as rather introspective, but I was probably more of a ruminator before meeting Alina. And for me, introspection is more effective when I can later verbalize it to someone else, almost like some kind of approval process validating my work.

Sometimes, when things were tough for either one or both of us, lunch breaks would turn into therapy sessions. While we always had a lot on our plates, literally and figuratively—at least I always piled up the food—we put a premium on these sessions, knowing they were probably the most helpful tool we had for getting through a difficult work environment. It was much better than just beating our heads against the wall and trying to solve our problems through brute force. We showed up for each other as best we could.

There were times when we both suspected one of us may not

make it much longer, but often, with creativity and perseverance, we found ways to improve our situation. So, as I was spending more time on fishing trips and having a harder time showing up mentally for my day job, it carried a lot of weight when she noticed.

At one point it became evident to me that I was still holding on to what this job was years ago, the pranks, the games, the camaraderie, and its success and fulfillment. I was refusing to acknowledge that everything had changed. I kept holding out hope for the good old days, but time doesn't move in reverse, and even the echoes were getting fainter each year.

Soon other people began noticing the same thing Alina did, and it was harder not to pay attention. Honestly, she was probably one of the biggest reasons I hadn't left yet; that and fear of change or plain old inertia. Without her friendship and support, I don't know how I would've made it through some of those days. At the same time, she was a link that tied me to my idealized version of what my career used to be but no longer was.

I needed to delineate my idealized version of the job with what reality was in the present. Likewise, I needed to differentiate between a convenient coworker friendship and something beyond that. She wasn't just a really good coworker; she was a really good friend, period, and that didn't have to end if my job did. Working with your friends is a nice perk if you can get it, but it's not a requirement.

I knew what I wanted to do at that point, but I wasn't sure I was ready. I needed to dip my toes in the water.

FAKE IT TILL YOU MAKE IT

I WASN'T sure how far I was going to take this yet, but over the last few months I had begun laying the groundwork to advertise a formal fishing guide service. I set up a website and uploaded all the fishy pictures I had on my phone. That's a big part of marketing a fishing service: catch a fish, take a photo. Always make sure the angle is right and the hands are behind the fish so the camera captures its full glory. Writing frequent fishing reports is smart for building credibility and website traffic. I was planning to use all my time off work for fishing trips and bring as many paying clients along as possible for a trial run.

By early June I was guiding my first group. I had my guiding license, insurance, First Aid and CPR training, the website, the gear, and a boat that I technically still shared with my dad, though he was more than happy for me to use it while exploring this guiding idea. I knew how to catch fish, and I'd taken other people fishing. This time, though, they were paying me. This time they had expectations. This time, I was supposed to be the expert, the fishing guide. As these thoughts ran through my head, I was about to meet them for breakfast at their lodge on the shore of Devils Lake, North Dakota, to discuss our plan of attack for the day.

I had fished plenty at Devils Lake and had my share of success. The previous year I posted a picture of a 30-inch, ten-pound walleye I caught in July with a couple buddies of mine, and Henry, a former co-worker of mine saw it. He said he'd been there the week before—and a few times the previous couple years—but had never caught fish like that. They did it alone a few days and hired guides a few days. They caught fish, but they wanted some bigger ones. Fast forward eleven months and I'm sitting with them at breakfast explaining how I think we're going to catch bigger ones.

On one hand, it was a good way to get my feet wet. I had worked with Henry at my first investment company. We'd had lunch together, worked on projects together, and had after-work drinks together. In fact, he and some other coworkers had once locked my phone in my drawer and called it while pretending to be talking to Microsoft tech support.

We got along quite well, so I wasn't going in completely cold. I also knew his dad, Henry Sr., because I had played at his annual poker tournament over a decade ago and took a cool grand on that victory. My hands still shake sometimes thinking about that drive home with $1,000 in cash in my pocket at age twenty-four.

On the other hand . . .

Two of the other guys on the trip were his uncle Howard (Henry Sr.'s older brother) and his uncle Randy on his wife's side. The fifth rounding out the group was Randy's stepson Dylan. As I sat down at the table, Henry Sr. looked me square in the eye with a look of expectation.

"So, you're our guide this year, huh?"

Later, Howard expressed frustration with last year's guide.

"That punk kid drove us all around that lake without hardly one goddamn bite all day!"

Tough crowd.

As much confidence as I had in Devils Lake and our prospects of getting on some fish, I had never seen it in the condition we found it that day. The weather had brought in a cold front—not great, as it breaks the early warming trend— and the water temps prefront were still cold for June after an unusually cold spring. The lake is normally full of algae blooms which cloud the water a bit and make for strong daytime fishing whereas in other lakes the walleye often thrive more in low-light situations given their unique characteristics. Their large eyeballs are designed to take in more light than their prey and predators, thus clear water on bright, sunny days can over-whelm their senses and postpone their hunting until more favorable times.

It takes warm temps for algae to grow, however, and the lake as this point was crystal-freaking clear. It was so clear, in fact, the first walleye I saw was actually under water, not in the boat, spooked out of a weed bed as I idled and it darted away.

As a result of their light sensitivity, you don't often catch walleyes that can see you. Normally I'm trolling by this time of year—using the boat to slowly pull baits through the water underneath us—but now we're forced into a shallow casting situation to get our baits further away from the boat, something I was not terribly comfortable with at that point.

One thing that can greatly help your chances in clear water conditions is wind. The waves refract the light more, breaking up the penetration and lowering visibility. The right amount can make walleyes much more catchable, but in the not-so-rolling, open plains of North Dakota, some wind can often turn into a gale.

The preponderance of evidence I've seen indicates Devils Lake got its name from a translation error. The natives were trying to tell the white dudes not to drink the water, that it was "bad water." Devils Lake is quite salty, especially when water levels are low. "Bad" was misinterpreted as "Devil," hence Devils Lake.

Some, however, claim it was named after its reputation for nasty waves and the number of unfortunate souls who had drowned falling through the ice during winter fishing.

At any rate, we got blown off the lake after three hours on day one.

This was perhaps a blessing in disguise. We only caught two fish, but what's a guy to do, right? It was almost unfishable. We were forced into spots the wind would *almost* allow, and even then, the waves stirred up the water in the shallow bay we fished so badly that crystal clear turned to a chocolate-milk swirl. As I drove around the mud pulling crankbaits with Randy and Dylan, my clients for that day's rotation, I asked, "What d'ya guys think?"

"I'll stay out here as long as ya want. I'm just chillin'," said Dylan in his shorts and tank top, relaxed as a spring breaker on the beach, impervious to the wind and not-so-warm air.

"We're kinda just pissin' in the wind here, aren't we?" said Randy.

"Yeah, basically" I admitted. "We might get one or two more if we're lucky, but it's gonna be tough."

"Let's get the hell outta here."

I had survived the day—even made a small tip of $40—but there were two more days to go. And with no wind excuses, I had to find a way to produce.

Given there were five of them in the group, Henry brought his own boat, and we rotated two of them into my boat each day. Dylan was joining me again for day two, along with Henry Sr. It wound up being another struggle. The wind was not quite as strong, but the temperatures were colder and the skies cloudier. We just couldn't get a lot of bites. That said, boats around us didn't seem to be doing much either. It was legitimate tough-bite conditions the way the weather changed and took the water temps in the wrong direction. I'm grateful my clients understood as much.

By the middle of the afternoon, thankfully, we stumbled into a pod of spawning white bass, and they were ravenous. They weren't the main target, but as tough as the walleyes were, Dylan was more than happy slamming sixty bass in an hour. It was darn near every cast! He rocked his backward hat and turned up his portable speaker channeling all his favorite music to rock those bass in a beatdown.

The few walleyes we had landed to this point were typically hitting casted lures, mostly crankbaits, tossed up shallow on wind-blown shorelines. We'd been dabbling in that method, but we hadn't stuck with it long enough. Most of this was my own lack of confidence in the technique, not only with guiding clients but even in my personal fishing capacity. Somehow, I had to commit to it and give my clients confidence it would work, even if it started slowly. Fake it till you make it, right?

Yet again, day three started off slowly, but sometimes these early season bites can heat up as the day goes on and the water warms. Howard and Randy were along with me this day, and eventually Howard hauled in a white bass. Something to keep momentum. Then a pike. Then I hit a walleye. Then we got a couple more 'eyes as we worked down the sandy shoreline. It wasn't fast and furious, but it was enough to keep interest. And while they occasionally hinted at moving spots or changing tactics, I told them we had to stick to our guns and it would pay dividends.

North Dakota's climate had become much wetter the past few decades, and the lake had no natural outlets. As a result, the already infamous Devils Lake rose uncontrollably, swallowing everything in its path. It became a bit of a nation-wide phenomenon written in many a newspaper article as roads, bridges, cornfields, and even railroad tracks became fishy playgrounds.

Eventually we reached one of these flooded railroad tracks, and the wind was pushing water into the corner where the track met the perpendicular shoreline. A good fisher person will keep a lookout for such spots as they corral life into a nice little smorgasbord for hungry predators. A few casts in, Randy hooked into a fish, and it started ripping some drag on his line. Until now we'd been catching 17-to-19-inch walleyes, solid fish, but they wanted bigger. This one was much bigger.

As the fish made runs under the boat, I talked him through it.

"Keep tension but let him pull if he pulls."

"Pick up slack when the fish takes a break."

"Keep your rod out wide to avoid him getting under the boat."

Eventually the fish came up, and I knabbed it with the net, all twenty-six inches of her! I don't know which emotions were stronger, his excitement or my sense of relief, but judging by the complete stoic face he maintained throughout the process, I would say mine.

"Great fish, Howard! I mean Randy! I get names confused when I get excited!"

Randy lifted the fish out of the net, still straight-faced.

"Hold that baby up so I can get your picture!" I said.

He began to raise the fish with its dorsal fin pointed in my direction.

"Rotate it a bit outward. Get your hand behind it and show that whole side to the camera so we can see just how big it is."

"Like this?"

"Perfect."

Snap.

It's incredible how one bite can change an entire trip. If you take away this fish, it wasn't much to write home about. But any time you pull in a trophy-caliber walleye, a client is going to remember. In twenty years, no matter how stoic he may have been, he'll remember that fish and that photograph. When I got back to my lodge later that night, I texted Dad that photo, and he said what he always says about a big fish: "That made the trip right there!" His response bombarded me with waves of validation.

To this day, I don't understand Randy's lack of reaction. I assume he just isn't a very excitable character. A few minutes after that catch-of-the-week, he had hooked into another similar caliber fish and wound up losing it as it ran under the boat and snapped the line. His reaction was almost indistinguishable from the previous catch. Nevertheless, after they invited me to their campsite for a fish fry that last evening, they seemed happy enough with the guide they'd hired.

Overall I was thrilled with this first true guiding experience, but my overriding feeling that night was relief. It was a massive exhale. I had a sense going in that this first trip wouldn't make my business, but it could break it, or at least break me. Had it gone poorly, I wonder if I would have lost my confidence and started second-guessing this venture.

It took a while to sink in. I stayed that night and fished myself the following day, casting lines and reliving the moments, how they felt and what they meant going forward. Until Randy's fish, I had survived; after it, I had thrived. I now felt this idea had strong legs underneath it. I'd dipped my toes in the water, and it felt great. How was I supposed to go back to work now?

GOETZ GETS ME ALL IN

AFTER COMPLETING my first official guiding trip at Devils Lake in early June, I took some more time off from the office in late June and early July to focus on Lake Sakakawea, the large Missouri River reservoir in North Dakota. If a guiding business was in the cards, Devils Lake had become a favorite destination of mine, but part of me truly missed reservoir fishing. Since Sakakawea was not quite three hours from Devils, I wondered if I could work both. My mind started to work full time on this part-time gig.

Of course, I was hoping to drum up some business while I was there, but if not, I would just do a lot of fishing, scouting, and video recording for my YouTube channel. As luck would have it, though, one of my guide friends whom I had met through email and phone, a mentor of sorts, got a call he was unable to fulfill and was kind enough to pass the client on to me.

The trip was organized by the father of the group and included his son, brother, and his own dad (Grandpa). Medicine was the most popular profession in this family by the last name of "Goetz," but the brother had chosen an investment theme to his real-world career same as I. Goetz is German, I would soon learn, and a very common name, like "Smith" or "Johnson" in English. Phonetically, it's pronounced "gets."

There were a few unique challenges about this upcoming gig. First and most obvious, it would be the first trip with complete strangers for customers. Second, it would include a full boat with four people plus myself, which portended a busy day to test my skills and patience. Third, it would be the first time I would have a young child along for the adventure, a boy of around ten.

The bite leading up to their day on the water was pretty good, a typical early-summer feeding binge. The only real challenge had been finding the better-quality fish. You could find a bunch of juveniles on certain spots, especially in eighteen to twenty-two feet of water. The more mature fish, the 18-to-22-inch class, were running a little shallower. Shorelines receiving the brunt of the wind and waves were a productive spot.

The churning water kicks up mud from Sakakawea's clay banks and forms a muddy blanket on the surface of the water. This provides a little protection from intense sunlight on the walleyes' sensitive light receptacles and a little camouflage to assist in ambushing their prey. Our presentation for attacking these fish was trolling bottom bouncers and spinners with night crawler harnesses in some fairly shallow water of about eight to fifteen feet, clear as mud, easy as walleye pie.

The group talked about having fairly extensive fishing experience, albeit a lot of it involved fly rods and trout streams, so I figured as long as I could keep the little guy in the water and out of snag trouble—and the fish were biting—it would be a pretty smooth day. At this point in my life, I had already learned fish could throw me curveballs. I was about to learn that clients could be equally unpredictable.

We hit the water a few minutes late due to a small, early rain shower, then the skies cleared off pretty well for us the rest of the day. They were prepared and pleasant, and we got along well from the start. The little boy was excited to be out on the water, as was Grandpa, and the two brothers seemed thrilled and relaxed just to be out of the office. I was hoping to capitalize on high spirits with a bunch of great fish catches.

Per the program, we started off fishing shallow with the bottom bouncers around a nice little point that stuck out into the water, seemingly a good place to get in the groove early. I explained the routine of baiting the line and letting the bottom bouncer down to the lake floor, knowing how much line to let out, and how to feel a bite as opposed to sand or rock. I figured fishing shallow water with less line out would make things easier.

About a minute into our first trolling pass, one of the guys gets caught up on the rocks, so we all real up, turn around, and free his line. We reset and start trolling again and quickly get a second snag. Then dad nests up his reel by letting down too fast.

After about twenty minutes on the spot, by the grace of the fishing gods, the little boy pulls in a nice 18-inch walleye, and soon we get a second. At that point, albeit with two fish landed, we're looking at two tangled reels and probably five snags, and my mind is scrambling to figure out how we can sustain a fishing day at this pace.

Grandpa was comically forgetful. Sometimes I would turn my head and find him waiting patiently, rod in hand, as the other three were already fishing. Other times, with his line actually in the water, I'd ask, "Have you checked your bait recently?" and he would reel up to show an empty set of hooks. Or sometimes he would reel up his line and show me two night crawlers, one on each hook, probably still fishable but not necessary or by design. This double crawler situation was a move repeated by the little boy a few times as well. I didn't buy enough bait for this!

One of the funniest gaffes, however, came from the invest-ment brother after he broke off one of two hooks on his crawler harness. For the visual of the reader, the setup we were using includes about five feet of fishing line, then a plastic snap swivel to which you can snap a spinner blade to let it rotate around your line, a few beads for color and spacing purposes, and then two hooks spaced about three inches apart, the first for the head of the night crawler, the second for the middle, and the tail would hang off the back as its pulled through the water.

When I saw he had lost the back hook, I simply threw him a tube of premade spinner rigs for him to replace his old rig in full. There's a snap swivel on the end of the bottom bouncer (bottom bouncer being the weight ahead of the rig) that would allow him to remove the old rig and attach the new one via the loop knot at the head of the line.

I went about my business doing guiding things when I heard him ask, "Do you have any shorter ones?" A little thrown off by the question, I replied, "What exactly do you mean by shorter ones?" At this point he showed me his handy work. He had attached an entire new rig to the snap swivel made for the spinner on the older rig, effectively making the setup twice as long as it was before instead of removing the old rig and attaching the new one clean. We all had a pretty good laugh once he realized what he was actually trying to do.

Again, I saw my dad in myself that morning making assumptions of others' knowledge. Given their claim to experience, my reaction was to not discredit their statement. I held back because I was afraid of talking down to them. Now I wondered if this was behind Dad's past assumptions about me as well. Perhaps he worried that pointing out seemingly obvious things would lead to me inferring I wasn't smart enough. He wasn't just making an error in omission, he was making an error in judgement, but he had reasoned it through in his head and made the best choice with the information he had. I think most of us are smart enough, really, which makes it worth giving anyone the benefit of the doubt.

Nevertheless, after a bit of a rough morning and moving to a cleaner spot with fewer snags, we had a decent number of fish in the livewell, and my group was starting to settle into the day. Around 1:00, the bite hadn't completely stopped, but it had slowed a touch, making room for us to sneak in a little lunch as we continued to drag our lines around the water. I started to relax, and they started to relax even more, taking in the scenery and trading memories about other fishing trips from their past. Then somebody got a little sleepy after filling their belly.

If I had given you three guesses, you'd probably only have a fifty-fifty shot at getting it right. Was it the little boy? No. Certainly then grandpa, right? Wrong again! The same poor brother who had struggled with his double rig situation just a little while before was sitting up in the front of the boat taking in the sun and being lulled to sleep by the gentle rocking of the waves. Eventually I looked forward and noticed that, while I can't see his eyes underneath his sunglasses, his facial expression looks a little more blank. And his posture is a little slumped. And his hands are barely gripping the fishing rod sitting loosely on his lap.

Instead of waking him up, I thought it would be more enjoyable to point this out to his brother and share a good laugh, which I most definitely did. Then looking back to Mr. Sleepy, I can see his rod start to bend over as his line gets bit by a fish. I leave my seat and lunge up toward the bow to grab the rod off of his lap, when he startles awake. I'm not sure if it was my movement or if he felt the bite, but he was sure as hell awake at this point and proceeded to set the hook and reel in another nice walleye.

Not all stories have happy endings, but this one did for Mr. Sleepy. First of all, he woke in time to keep that literal "fish of his dreams" and the rod I thought might wind up at the bottom of the lake. Minutes after that sleep-induced chaos, he also landed our biggest catch of the day, a nice 22-inch walleye, zero to hero in less than a full-trolling pass.

In total, I believe we kept sixteen walleyes between seventeen and twenty-two inches. We also released a series of smaller ones that weren't fit for the dinner table quite yet, along with some white bass, smallmouth bass, and northern pike. We had called it a day after about six hours of fishing as the sun and the waves were starting to take their toll on the young boy. He was super revitalized by the time we reached the cleaning station, though, and attentively watched and helped in the process of cutting their catch into nice, tidy fillets for them to take home.

As they're getting ready to depart for the day, Mr. Sleepy came over to me and offered some words of advice.

"This investment world that we are both in is just a soul sucker. You're good at this guiding thing. If you're really thinking about doing this full time, I say just go for it, man."

He then handed me a generous tip for my day's work, and we all said our goodbyes.

On the way back from the marina, I called my dad.

"I just spent all day untangling messed up rods, baiting hooks, rerigging broken lines, and getting them out of snags. And it was one of the best days of my life."

JUST BROTHERS

MY BROTHER and I are about to go on stage at a local open mic joint in downtown Des Moines, Iowa. Yes, we have other interests and hobbies outside of fishing. We have our guitars in hand and a small set list, "Walking in Memphis" from Mark Cohen and "Let Her Cry" from Hootie and the Blowfish. As we approach the stairs to the stage, the guy who is supposed to introduce us asks through the microphone, "What are you guys called?"

My brother looks at me like a fellow student who didn't expect this question to be on the test. I shrug and say, "I don't know, we're just brothers."

Immediately thereafter, my brother's friend back in the audience shouts out, "Yeah! Just Brothers!" and starts clapping and hollering loudly.

After the show, I told my brother that if we did any real gigs, Just Brothers should be our name. He looked at me with that face of his that says "I'm not gonna say 'no,' but I'm not going to approve either." Super wasted opportunity in my view.

∽

Brandon and I are brothers, but we aren't "just brothers." He never said as much, but I wonder if this was his hesitation. Or perhaps he was just not wanting to lock himself into a band name and give me the impression we were going to start hammering out bigger set lists and going on tour.

I don't know if this holds true for all children, but when our parents got divorced, I think we got much tighter. With all the change around us, we were each other's constant. We looked out for each other, we helped each other through it, and we had one extremely deep shared experience. In many ways we were also best friends. Sure, we picked on each other, and sure he intensified the picking when he got into his early "too-cool-for-high-school" stage, but on the whole, I wouldn't trade our brotherly relationship for anything.

Our two main differences are in our physical stature and our personality type. He did not inherit as much of the Bloemendaal archetype as I did. He is much shorter and leaner, and he unfortunately inherited male-pattern baldness from our mom's side. He's played this card well, however, now in his thirties rocking a shaved head and a thick beard. With a pair of sunglasses, he bears a striking resemblance to Chris Daughtry. Swapping the sunglasses for a hat, he bears a passing resemblance to Aaron Rodgers of the Green Bay Packers.

I love to get everyone marching to the same beat, singing in harmony and rising up in concert to make one beautiful whole better than the parts. Brandon marches to his own very unique drummer, and often times I'm not sure he even hears the music everyone else is playing. On our brothers-only vacations to destinations like Puerto Rico and South Beach Miami, this occasionally led to disagreements about what to do when, but it also gave us the opportunity to see twice as many of the local eating establishments since we were almost never in sync with our hunger clocks.

We make each other better by showing each other alternative views and challenging each other's ideas rather than simply agreeing with one another. The one thing we always agree about, however: we should probably go fishing.

I will admit at times I can be a bit of a fish snob. If I'm not on a boat at a lake full of healthy walleyes, I can sometimes grow disgruntled and start wishing I was somewhere else. My brother, however, will attend any all-you-can-eat fish buffet and catch them in any way possible, from the boat, through the ice, or from shore. Even on trips when we do have the boat in tow, Brandon won't hesitate to grab a weapon of choice and head down to the dock to try his luck there before we even set out on the boat. His philosophy: "Cast a liiiiine!"

Of course, he did not invent this phrase, but he popularized a specific use of it within our family on a guys' trip to Leech Lake the first year Dad and I owned our new boat. It was the three of us joined by our younger brother Tyler and we were sampling some fare different from our typical Missouri River familiarity. We horribly mistimed the seasons, booking the trip a couple of weeks too early during an unseasonably warm fall, so the fishing was terrible. The trip itself, however, was one of my favorites.

We were sitting in our cabin one night after having not caught anything worth writing home about, and Tyler was debating whether or not to get on Tinder since he was starting to reach an appropriate dating age. Brandon simply looked at him and said, "Cast a line!" Tyler, obsessed with perfecting all one-liner jokes, repeated the phrase a minimum of a hundred times over the next few days. Even though he may have worn it out vocally, it still stands as a wonderful metaphor for fishing and life in general.

Brandon has a soft spot for simple and efficient lyrics. He is more of a poet than a wordy rambler. We've often had conversations about ourselves and the fact that, if anything holds us back in life, it's often our lack of confidence to follow through with a decision. Cast a line. Just go do the thing. It became a mantra of sorts in addition to its status as a simple dating joke.

Tyler took this to heart in more ways than one. As he got

into high school, he and his friends started getting into heavy metal music, buying guitars, figuring them out, and eventually writing their own songs. They were one hundred percent self-taught. They put together a demo CD and started playing small shows around the area. Their mantra was "Just do the thing." Cast a line, if you will.

If I'm an introvert—and I am—Tyler is the poster child for our species. But when he was playing his guitar on stage, he was in a different world. It was almost as if someone else possessed his body, maneuvered it onto stage, and shredded metal like fire. He was absolutely fearless up there. He was not afraid of screwing up or embarrassing himself; he knew failure was part of the process. Just do the thing.

As years went by and discussions continued within the family about a fishing guide service, I started to think a lot about my little brother Tyler. Was I keeping myself from doing something I truly wanted simply because of a lack of confidence? Because of a fear of failure? Was I too afraid to just "do the thing?" Maybe it was I who needed to cast a line, literally and figuratively.

Three of my closest friends helped solidify that thought. The four of us met freshman year of college and lived on the same floor. Each one of them became roommates of mine at different times during and after school. They were like brothers in a different sense of the word—in every way except by blood.

In July 2019, our little college crew got together to witness and take part in the wedding of one of our "brothers." It was a bit of a low-key event, and not typical of the reception dance parties we attended for the weddings of the other two guys, probably a sign of our ever-increasing age. There was a courtyard area outside the hotel with a series of fire pits and comfortable lawn chairs, and the three of us not getting married that day decided to have a fireside chat and catch up. As we got to the topic of my career and fishing, one of the guys offered this:

"There's only one thing holding you back from what I can

tell. You simply struggle to get out of your comfort zone. You're done with your current job; you've been done for a long time. We can all tell that. I get why you're staying, and no one could blame you, but sometimes you gotta get out of your own comfort zone."

He was right. And so was Brandon. It was all about confidence and comfort zones. What would happen if I were to just cast a line? And what would I do in this world without my brothers? They aren't just brothers; they're so much more.

IF NOT NOW, WHEN?

IT WAS ONLY JULY, and I was already starting to push my luck with time off work. We had recently gotten away from paid time off and switched to a so-called flex-time model, so there supposedly wasn't an official counting of days. Still, I know there are always unwritten rules. I had two more groups asking if they could take fishing trips for the fall. In the midst of starting a new business, even if it was just a side gig, I really didn't want to turn them away. It's a good problem to have, but it's a problem nonetheless. I decided to do the prudent thing—ask my boss for another week off. I planned to bring it up at my next one-on-one chat with him, which would end up getting rescheduled a few times due to "unexpected events."

I actually thought there was a chance he would allow it. My boss was somewhat low-key, and he also enjoyed fishing, so perhaps he could empathize. Plus, the major project I believed I had been earmarked to work on continued to get pushed off further into the distance, much like the scheduling discussion I was supposed to have with my boss. All the Waffle Houses in the country don't have enough grease for the wheels of Corporate America.

Eventually we did sit down to talk. No dice. He said he just couldn't justify another week off with management. "It seems I have a decision to make," I said to myself mentally, and then he said the same thing out loud. He substituted "you" for "I," though, of course.

I really didn't think I was going to be at this crossroads so soon. My first year attempting to run the guide service as a side business and already I found myself considering the boldest of moves.

There are always things in life we feel we literally can't wait for. The first trip to Disney World. Your grade school friends to arrive so you can finally open your birthday presents. Evidently, according to TV commercials, cheese baked into the crust of the pizza. Dessert for people who think it's appropriate to order dessert before the main meal, a truly psychotic bunch, if you ask me. Seriously, where does it end? Chronology has a very important place in life. There's a reason we get dressed *before* going to work.

The thing was, if I stayed in the job, not only were my guiding trips over for the year, but so were my personal ones. I was fresh out of time. I barely had enough to make a trip for a family Christmas, or anything else for that matter. I was anxious just thinking about it.

Anxiety. The word had taken on a whole new meaning that year. I was officially diagnosed with anxiety as a medical condition by my primary care doctor. A job I was once good at, even somewhat looked forward to, was becoming so stressful and so void of purpose that even a poorly-worded email from a colleague could damn near give me a heart attack.

I was in the hospital for a few days during the winter. My body was not responding super well to the situation. I was struggling more with the excessive sitting during the day. I desperately wanted to get out and move. I was having more gut problems, possibly a result of the anxiety. Muscle aches and tension were becoming almost unbearable. And for the first time in my life, I was having very regular headaches, even migraines on occasion.

My legs weren't doing very well. I had a hard time standing for any length of time. When I did stand, they got super achy, and I got super tired. My heart would start to beat extremely fast, and I would easily become short of breath. A couple times I passed out, which is how I wound up at the hospital. I was there for almost three days the second time and sat through a series of tests of my heart and brain looking for rhythm issues and possible stroke issues. I had a bunch of bloodwork done as well.

The last and most unique exam was called a tilt table test. They strap you to a hospital bed and tilt you up almost vertically and see how your heart rate responds and whether or not you lose consciousness. I stayed awake, but after about ten minutes my heart rate went from sixty to over one hundred beats per minute as my face got pale as a corpse and I began to feel miserable just as I did when I stood for too long.

"You doin' okay?" I remember the nurse saying as she watched with her clipboard tracking my heartrates and physical condition.

"I've been better." I felt like a science experiment. The doctor occasionally walked by to watch as well, taking sips of his iced coffee.

"Just a few more minutes."

I was eventually diagnosed with postural orthostatic tachycardia syndrome, or POTS for short. It's a disorder of the autonomic nervous system which controls things without our conscious action, things like breathing, heart pumping, etc. Taken literally, POTS means your heart beats really fast when you stand. As to why it happens, essentially all the blood pools in my legs and my vessels don't do their job of squeezing it back up to the heart, so my heart works overtime to try to get the blood back up.

There are two possible reasons this could've occurred. First, it could be part of an autoimmune reaction. It could also be a side effect of anxiety, my body pumping out too much adrenaline, which shunts the blood to the extremities. When this goes on too long, my circulatory system fails to return the blood back up to my heart and my brain.

My prescriptions wound up being an increased salt intake—to up my blood pressure, a remedy no one argues with but few are allowed—proper hydration, and a small dose of a kidney hormone medication usually prescribed for Addison's disease to encourage the kidneys to retain sodium in the blood. They also gave me long, tight socks up to my thighs to squeeze the blood back up, which are not entirely comfortable. It did all work to a degree, however, especially when I had to be in inside and stationary at work.

What seemed to help even more, though, was being outside, moving around, breathing fresh air, and getting sunlight on my skin. It felt good for my body, and it felt great for my soul. It started to feel like my body was trying to tell me something. I'd done a lot of things in the previous few years to improve my health status, and they all seemed to work to some degree, but I couldn't quite get over the hump.

I've come to think of these autonomic nervous system disorders as disconnect-from-nature disorders. All those things it's supposed to regulate automatically, like blood pressure, heart rate, and breathing rate, have a rhythm to them. Perhaps nature is our metronome or a conductor, and without nature, it has a hard time staying in sync. It's only a theory. I'm no doctor, but it seems to work that way for me.

The all-knowing "they" collective also says the mind is a powerful thing; what you think can somehow manifest itself into reality. Was it possible my anxiety and lack of purpose was also manifesting itself in my physical and medical problems? Or was I just looking for an excuse to fish every day? Was I looking for the easy way out, to just cut and run?

The more I explored these ideas, the less it seemed to be the latter. Leaving an extremely well-paying corporate job with a retirement account and health insurance to go it alone and start my own fishing business is certainly not "taking the easy way out." If anything, it's a massive risk and, in financial terms, an extremely stressful one. But internally, it seemed as though it came with a lot less emotional resistance. As scary as the idea sounded, it was a different sort of fear, and it didn't cause any anxiety. Thinking about what would happen to me and my health if I stayed in my current job, however, gave me immense amounts of anxiety.

The more I thought about it, the more the idea of even two more weeks, the standard notice for resigning, began to seem almost unbearable. Beyond just not wanting to be there, it was the thought of what I wasn't doing when I was there. Whether it was an anxiety attack or not, I literally felt like I had a hard time breathing. I felt like a fish out of water lying on the beach surrounded by all of this perfectly good oxygen it simply couldn't use.

Around that same time, I had been getting reacquainted with a band I thoroughly enjoyed in my college years: Incubus. While listening to their older records, already familiar to me, I decided to check whether or not they had come out with any newer music I hadn't yet discovered. In 2011, it turns out, they'd put out a record titled *If Not Now, When?* Well played, universe. Well played.

I started to take the question seriously. If I didn't do this now, when the momentum was building and I had clients continuing to ask for trips, when would I ever do it? Would I ever do it?

I'm not necessarily a believer in fate, but it does seem possible that life occasionally presents you with opportunities fitting for a situation, and if you don't take them in that fleeting moment when they're available, you might never have the chance again. It almost seemed like I didn't have a choice or I had already made up my mind before I asked the question.

The hard part of this life-altering "decision" was just

acknowledging what I already knew. Suffering comes from knowing something and refusing to acknowledge it and take a new course in response. All I had to do was let go.

I scheduled another chat with my boss. The conference room where our team conducted such chats was right behind our row of cubicles. It always feels a little odd walking into one of those in front of coworkers wondering if your body language or facial expression telegraphs the topic. I always tried walking in there with a poker face, whether it mattered or not, but on that particular day I'm sure others had an inkling of what was happening. As I closed the door behind us, he got right to it.

"This must be about the fishing thing, huh? What are you thinking?"

I was shaky physically, both out of excitement and at the prospect of communicating big change to someone, but I was resolute.

"I need to give it a chance. I can't look back and wonder."

He smiled. "I kinda figured that was the answer. It's pretty exciting. I'm happy for ya."

We then hashed out some administrative details. He stood up and opened the door. I walked out a changed man whether my face said so or not.

We landed on a four-week transition, which did seem quite daunting because I had really wanted to get started on this immediately having made the decision, but I had given them my word I would do what was necessary to leave properly. My last official day with the company would be August 26, 2019. We told our small team later that week. Two weeks later a notice was sent to the broader departments around the company.

Honestly, I wasn't sure how my coworkers would react. I knew some of them might be a little sad I was leaving because they may have enjoyed our working relationship, but I wasn't sure if they would support my reasons for leaving. I expected a fair amount of "Oh . . . are you sure you really want to do this?"

What actually happened quite surprised me. Many were

actually jealous (or at least said they were). Some of the conversations I had led me to believe others had pondered leaving as
well but didn't know how. Some people said they were proud of
me. Some people said they were excited for me. And a few of
them said, "Once you leave, you'll never look back." There was a
lot of talk about "following-your-passion" and related clichés,
and apparently most people have a lot of respect for that sort of
thing.

I wasn't sure which made people more likely to respond in
this manner, the fact they were unhappy with their own job or
admiration for the "following-your-passion" part. Nevertheless,
it felt good to know I wasn't the only one going through it. I also
felt guilty my life situation set me up to make this decision while
other people simply didn't have the same set of circumstances.

I wasn't married, I didn't have children, and I had been fairly
diligent about my finances and savings. I already owned the boat
and much of the equipment I was about to use. Outside of
leaving my secure salary, I didn't have a lot else holding me back.
I was only responsible for myself. It's not that I owed any of
those people anything, but somehow it gave me more resolve to
succeed in this endeavor, if only to show other people it can be
done.

There were a handful of people, in a very lighthearted way,
who called my move "early retirement," insinuating I was retiring
from my career to go fishing every day. This wasn't the way I saw
it at all. To me it was a mission to find a way to support myself
financially on my own terms doing something I loved and
sharing it with others.

In essence, this is why I had contemplated leaving for so long
already. There wasn't a lot of joy for me in investments anymore.
I didn't feel like I was helping anyone, not in any meaningful
way. It's one thing to work hard and put in long hours for something you care about, for something you think changes other
people's lives for the better. All that stress winds up having a
reward at the end. But if you take away the reward and the

purpose and leave only the stress, the inevitable result is burnout.

Granted, you are still being compensated for this work, but the heart doesn't recognize money as compensation. The heart needs purpose and validation. These can come in many different forms. Perhaps for some money works. For me it didn't.

Not surprisingly it was a religious friend of mine who, upon learning of this career move of mine, shared a fable that illustrates the power of perspective.

A man is walking down the street and happens upon a construction site with three bricklayers busy at work. When he asks them what they're building, the first says, "I'm building a wall." The second says, "I'm building a church!" with a little more happiness in his voice. The third says with serene joy, "I'm building a house of God!"

Religious or not, I think it gets the point across. Sounds like something my grandpa would have said too. If he's looking down at me now, I think he's smiling. Not that a fishing business is akin to building a literal house of God, but, you know. He just wants me to be happy.

In the midst of making my final rounds through the office, I went by Alina's floor to chat. Not that we wouldn't talk again fairly soon anyway, but still it seemed appropriate. We exchanged words for a while, and then I started to get sentimental, as I'm known to do with any level of "good-bye," causing an awkward silence that she soon broke.

"I'm gonna talk to you plenty anyway. Let's not make this weird."

We both grinned and went on our way. I would've asked for a hug, but I'd learned my lesson.

The next day I was outside, barefoot, watering the grass while talking on the phone to my new lawyer.

"So, I got your message here from my assistant saying you want to set up an LLC?"

"Yessir."

"And you're offering a fishing charter, is that right?"

"You got it."

"Alright, just pulling up some forms here. How's your day going, by the way?"

"It's great, actually. I'm working barefoot in my yard right now. Yesterday was my last day at the corporate office."

"No kidding? Wow! That's great. That must be very liberating."

"Without a doubt it is! I love my new office."

"Ha! I bet. Okay, and what did you want to name the entity?"

"Bloemedaal Guide Service, LLC."

THIS IS EVERYTHING NOW

I KNEW I might have to find work to make ends meet during the winter, but when I arrived in North Dakota in early September, I decided I was only going to think about fishing until mother nature said otherwise. I would attempt to pick up as many fall clients as I could, and the rest of the time would be spent learning every inch of massive Sakakawea, making videos for the YouTube channel, and building a name for myself and my business.

Fishing-wise, it was a tough time of year to begin, but I had to start somewhere. The lake and the fish were in transition from summer to fall, and there wouldn't be a strong bite until things started to cool down. But I was okay with that.

I spent the rest of my fishing year at a bed-and-breakfast near Deepwater Bay on Lake Sakakawea. I had the basement room in the main house for $40 a night. It's not much, but it was all I needed. The walls smelled like an old farmer's overalls, and the bubbly paneled floors moved and creaked. The artwork had an old west feel, that of true cowboys who used to roam the land and lasso four-legged, horned animals. At least it's authentic, and the location was perfect.

The people who run the place are blast-from-the-past-style,

conservative ranch folk, and they are sweet as the day is long. I had another companion as well. Their dog Bo, a fluffy old lab, had taken quite a liking to me, showing up at the door of my vehicle every night when I returned from the lake. We had discussions about fishing, whether he enjoyed them or not, though I suspect he was mostly into the attention and the petting. He and the homestyle breakfasts filled out any gaps the lake and the fish couldn't. The home-cooked bacon, eggs, and sausage in the morning reminded me of the fishing trips of my youth. Given my revised diet, French toast, however, was relegated to nostalgia.

Outside of fishing, so much was undefined, be that my future or just any given day on the water. Normally this would be a source of stress for me, yet it helped me stay in the present moment.

Though fishing was technically a job at that point, the days out on the lake scouting by myself were rather therapeutic. It took a while to decompress and let go, but it was the best medicine I knew. Each and every day, launching the boat and bucking the waves out to the main lake, I settled into myself and my surroundings. Hardening my confidence in my decision, I spent my days driving, graphing, marking waypoints, and catching a few fish along the way. Some of them inevitably become dinner, and occasionally I shared a feast with my housemates.

By the end of September, I managed to secure some business, but the location happened to be at Devils Lake again, nearly a three-hour drive from where I was staying. The travel and motel costs would eat into my profits, but that fall was about building a business, so the opportunity was still very much welcomed.

I went to the lake a day early to get in a little scouting and get a feel for the bite. Lots of fish were being caught, surprising for this early in the fall, but many of them were also fairly small, in the 13-to-15-inch range. Nevertheless, the first priority in guiding is getting action, which wasn't looking to be a problem.

My upcoming group was technically a couple of strangers,

but they were the husband and a friend of my SomaYoga instructor. One of them was a real estate agent who struck you as the type more than capable of carrying your new refrigerator up the stairs and into your kitchen. He had quite the charismatic smile and the outgoing personality you would expect of someone in his business. He was very bold and unapologetic, a bit of a modern day, real-life Gaston, if you don't mind the Disney reference. I imagine whatever group he ran with in high school, he was its center of attention and the focal entertainer. Reminded me a lot of my father, actually. I hope I didn't slip up and call him "Dad" too many times.

His buddy, a true partner in crime, moonlights as a bassist and vocalist for one of the best cover bands I've ever heard. I hadn't recognized him until they brought it up, but I had seen his band play at the state fair years prior back in Iowa. The two of them had quite the rapport, at least thirty percent rooted in *Dumb and Dumber* quotes, so we got off to a great start. "Tractor beam, rrrvvvt, sucked me right in."

I was feeling good about things, but the day wound up being a total farce. The weather was awful, wind blowing near thirty miles per hour, spitting rain at times, and temperatures around forty degrees. Thankfully, my cofishermen were hardened outdoor types and primed for adventure despite the challenge.

With the wind blowing the way it was, we didn't have a lot of options. There's one boat ramp in the back of a small bay protected enough to launch. It has at least a couple miles of shoreline on the calm side that was somewhat fishable, and I'd had success there before.

As we got the boat in the water and I turned on my Humminbird fish finder, I noticed I didn't have an accurate depth reading. I fidgeted with the monitor and the cables, but no luck. My mind began racing with worry about the first impression with my clients. As much as I didn't want to get wet in the cold and wind, I took off my jacket, rolled up my sleeves, and stuck my arm down into the frigid water up to my shoulder to play with the transducer, the probe which was supposed to be beaming images of the lake bottom to my screen if working properly. Much to my dismay, I found it simply dangling there instead of secured on the mounting bracket.

I wouldn't put all the pieces together until after our outing, but loading in rough water the previous day, I had apparently gotten the boat off center enough on the trailer that the mounting bracket hit one of the rollers and snapped right off.

Stuck in a part of the lake anything but my first choice and feeling a bit naked without functioning electronics, I scrambled to put something together to keep the guys in the game until I could regroup. We managed a few small walleyes on live bait, but nothing we could even put in the livewell. I resorted to trolling crankbaits on a large rock reef and hoped we could luck into something. The underwater terrain we fished was relatively flat, so my lack of depth reading wasn't as much of a hinderance.

The day's tone was light early; clients typically give you some grace knowing you have a full day to produce. As hours pass, however, grace always starts to fade to disappointment. And then I almost sensed a little bit of pity. They must have thought they could be doing better having rented their own boat, and it's possible they would have.

I was fortunate they were able to hook into a few good northern pike around the 30-inch mark, and they actually liked keeping and eating these fish. Not all clients do, as walleye is much more popular table fare, but with some oil and batter, perhaps a little tartar sauce, they're both worth eating. At that size they put up a hell of a fight and carry a lot of meat, too, so it was a small victory. I still felt confident that if the weather gave us a break and I could get my transducer fixed, we could have a good second day, but I definitely had an uphill battle in front of me to win back their trust.

I spent a good chunk of the night patching the transducer bracket with a liquid welding compound my clients recommended to me. Fishing comes naturally, but my mechanical skills need work. I hoped it would be strong enough to hold for one good fishing day until I could buy a brand-new bracket.

My lodge motel for those days was only a few doors down from my clients'. As I worked, I occasionally glanced over at Gaston regaling fellow lodge guests at a picnic table, pipe in one hand, brew in the other, as jolly and demonstrative as a human can be. I smiled and thought to myself, "When we get on some good fish tomorrow, it's gonna be a hell of a great time."

The next morning arrived with renewed optimism and a little reprieve from the wind. I met the guys as they were returning from the restaurant, just a short walk from our rooms. They were armed with a map and a bunch of tips from the locals. Shit. My clients were about to guide me.

The spot they were being directed toward was a bridge neck-down area between two bigger bodies on the lake. At this time of the year, oxygen content is lower in supply, and the current squeezing through these bottlenecks amplifies oxygen levels and draws in the food chain. The catch, however, is you need wind blowing in the proper direction to push the water through these bottlenecks. The bridge they—or their breakfast friends, rather —wanted to fish would've been great with the previous day's wind, but there was another, better option I wanted to fish on this day.

"Here's the deal," I said, "my goal is certainly to fish one of those bridges, at least to start. I wanted to yesterday as well, but I also didn't want to be stuck with that as our only option in all that wind. And with it blowing another direction, there's a better one we can hit today. There's also a good spot near there we can troll for some bigger fish. I know yesterday sucked, but you gotta trust me on this one. We'll get 'em."

"Alright," Gaston said. "We'll follow our guide!"

We absolutely killed it that day. It might've been one of the best days of walleye fishing I'd ever had for both numbers and size. We fished the bridge jigging up sixty walleyes, a couple pike, and a bunch of white bass. Some of the 'eyes were small, but we also had plenty of good eaters in the 16-to-18 -inch range as well. Even better, we only ever saw one or two boats there all day. Perhaps thirty-eight degrees of cold air and spitting rain kept everyone else inside by the fireplace.

"This is why we hired a guide!" said Gaston.

His buddy mentioned multiple times that he didn't think he'd ever caught so many fish in one day. It was only 11:00 a.m. Even after the first five walleyes came in, I had a massive weight lifted off my shoulders. After the sixtieth, I was floating.

The bite on the bridge eventually died down after two and a half hours. We boated just north where I knew of a deep old sunken road that used to skirt the outside of the lake before water levels rose. We were trolling crankbaits in about twenty-five feet of water, and I told the guys we had a possibility of getting some nicer fish there.

The bite wasn't quite as fast as the jig bite at the bridge, but over the next couple hours we pulled in six walleyes between twenty-one and twenty-three inches. What was already a great day had almost become epic. With the fish playing their part, the mood of the day was a total 180 from the previous debacle, even though we were getting rained on much of the time. It was like fishing with some old pals.

What I loved most about this group of guys was how much fun they had catching anything, any species, any size. We were also able to flip each other a lot of shit for missing bites we should've caught and catching fish that were a little horizontally challenged. At one point Gaston caught an infant of a seven-inch walleye and held it out toward my phone camera as far as his arms would allow, face serious as a heart attack, spoofing the optical trick that many fisher people use to make their catch just a little bit bigger than reality would allow.

At the end of the fishing day, I asked them to hold their four biggest fish at the cleaning station for a few photos and then surprised them by switching to video.

"You're on video now, by the way."

They both laugh.

"Say something funny."

Gaston turns his brain gears for a half second, then starts in:

"Um . . . so, this one is named the same as that one. It's the second cousin to that one so really it kinda goes like this," he says as he reorders the fish according to name or genealogy or something.

Mark quips, "I have no idea what any of that meant."

Neither did I, but it made me laugh anyway.

It was a true, all-around fishing experience, exactly what I wanted to achieve for anyone else kind enough to brave my vessel in the future. I felt like a true fishing guide. This was everything now. I got this.

WEATHERING THE STORM

AFTER THAT SPECTACULAR turn of events at Devils Lake, a defining moment in the infancy of my fishing career, it seemed nothing could bring me down. Besides, who's tall enough to even reach the ninth cloud? Oh, right. Mother nature, you and your earthly wingspan are a real buzzkill.

Upon returning to Sakakawea, we were bludgeoned with a snow and ice storm that felt two months too early for the first week in October. The temperatures dropped into the twenties, and I wouldn't be back on the water for at least four days. I had picked up two more client bookings, but they were promptly canceled. Now what?

I definitely wanted to stay. Even if I didn't do any more guiding, I wanted to do more fishing. The fall season can be epic for some really big walleyes, and if I could put together one good video for my YouTube channel, it could be a huge marketing moment to propel my business into the next season. After two days, and $80 more in lodging fees, I really started to question how long I could hold out.

The first day or two I kept myself busy with fishing reports and video editing, but those old farmhouse walls were closing in hard. I made a couple of trips out of town to keep from going stir crazy, but white-knuckling my Jeep across icy roads in heavy winds wasn't exactly a stress reliever. As I kept obsessively checking weather forecasts, I held onto the refrain "Only two more days. Only one more day." On October 7, despite temps in the low thirties and winds predicted at twenty miles per hour, I finally decided to dump the boat back in the water.

There was still snow on the banks, but the lake was wet. The water temps had dropped to more favorable fall fishing conditions in the mid-to-low fifties, but it would likely take the walleyes a few days to adjust after such an abrupt shift. Nevertheless, it wouldn't keep me from trying.

As I made my way from the marina out of the bay toward the main lake, it seemed to me the wind was picking up much more strongly than predicted. As it turned out, the gusts peaked at forty-five miles per hour! The bay was somewhat protected as the wind was blowing away from shore, but by the time I decided fishing was futile and returned to the marina, the wind was still strong enough to create havoc even on the calm side.

I reached the loading dock, grabbed my rope with one end fastened to the bow of my boat, and jumped out onto the dock. Even so, the wind started pushing my boat away from me so fast I suddenly shook in panic, questioning my ability to hold onto it. I could not believe how hard the wind was pushing my boat away from my outstretched arms, and for a few moments, I thought she was a goner. I hunkered down, using all of my 205 pounds as a low center of gravity, and pulled as hard on that rope as I'd ever pulled on anything before.

Finally, I got it secured to the dock's side and close enough to the post to tie the other end. One crisis averted.

I had launched at a different location this day, theoretically to get out of the wind. The ramp there was super steep, and the water that had dripped from the trailer in the morning was now frozen on the ramp as I attempted to load. After backing the trailer in and getting the boat latched up, I went around to my four-wheel-drive Jeep to get that sucker up on dry land.

As I eased onto the gas and off the break, I noticed I wasn't making much progress. And then occasionally I would slip backwards. Again, I started to panic, as there was not a single soul on site. At this point I was completely at the mercy of an icy boat ramp and four Jeep tires I had to trust to get the job done.

To be straight-up honest with you, I was lucky that day. After a couple of minutes, I slowly inched my way up the ramp to the point where I got some drier concrete and more traction. I should've brought along some ice melt or sand, things I will no doubt remember for future reference, but this hadn't crossed my mind as I'd never before fished below thirty-two degrees. Again, my season had almost ended early, this time to elements beyond my control rather than my own decision-making process.

The next few days the temperatures became more favorable —40s instead of 20s and 30s—and I continued scouting and learning, waiting for the epic fall moment I had stuck it out for over the last week. With the bite still not great, I spent more time mapping new areas, still filming, but making it less of a priority. Three days or so after launching in icy conditions, the fish started adjusting to the cold snap, and I picked off a few nice ones in these scouting areas. I decided the next morning I would head back to my prime locations near Deepwater Bay and see if the fish were ready for film.

As the sun rose, I was optimistic about a reprieve from the wind, but again it kicked up early and stronger than I'd hoped. The fish weren't yet cooperating either. I remember looking at my gauges and seeing the water temps right at fifty-one degrees, thinking it should be perfect for a great fall bite, but it just wasn't happening yet. The wind then started to wreak havoc on all the spots I wanted to fish. I was once again stuck on the calm side, hopelessly dragging around crankbaits with little to show for it.

I got two nice walleyes, some thick fish in the 20-to-23-inch range reminding me of what was out there, but it was very sporadic. During the afternoon, I managed some really nice pike close to forty inches in length, which were great pike even if not the target species! Fish are fish, and big ones make for good video, but I'm still searching.

I tucked underneath a large bluff for some wind protection to eat my lunch of cold, leftover fish and potatoes while watching some Dakota rancher's cattle on the shore stare back and "moo" at my presence. Or perhaps they were saying "mooooove." I don't know. Dr. Dolittle I am not. Ignoring the cows, I continued checking the hourly forecast, but it looked as though the wind was going to hold out like this until dark. Damn near ready to wave the white flag, I started looking ahead to tomorrow.

Perhaps it was divine intervention or just the usual difficulties weather folks have at predicting the future, but at around 4:30 in the afternoon, the wind almost completely laid down. I started looking away from the shoreline where I had been stuck for hours and noticed the whitecaps were gone. Now that the wind had been pounding the other shoreline for the entire day, I knew there was a good chance some big fish might move in there to feed on whatever the wind churned up.

I ran across the lake and started trolling crankbaits at the mouth of the bay where I had left off in the morning. I was running my lures in twenty-eight feet of depth on the edge of a sharp break where it fell quickly to much deeper water. It didn't all happen at once, but soon enough a 20-inch walleye pulled back on my bait and reluctantly found the bottom of my net. Another fifteen minutes later, another pullback, a feistier fish, and by the time it became visible and nettable, I got a look at a thick 23-inch eyeball. By 5:00, it started to have the feeling of something pretty special.

Soon it was hard to keep them off the line. Another 23-inch

fish, a 24-inch fish, and then I put away my second rod to simply focus on the one. The sun was going down, burning the blue horizon into a fiery reddish orange, and the fish were taking notice. I started catching them shallower, 25 feet, 22 feet, 18. The graph started to load up with more and more fish each time I passed through the spot. They were moving in for the evening kill.

Conditions were perfect, and I had complete control over the boat as even residual waves had now ceased. Even better, there wasn't another soul in sight. I had the spot, even the lake, all to myself. I had maybe thirty minutes of sunlight remaining. The bites were coming fast, but it all seemed to unfold in slow motion. I felt as though I could stretch each second as far as it could reach on a day that I wanted to last for eternity. As the fish got more aggressive, I decided to put away the trolling rods and drop down a snap jigging bait for hand-to-hand combat. Barely a minute later, I'm hooked up again.

Though my GoPro had died, my iPhone still made for a great camera sitting on the dash of my boat since there was nary a wave to knock it into the water or even distort the picture. The fish put up a hard fight, but soon enough I netted another fat 23-inch walleye. I showed it off the camera, blabbed a few words, released the fish, and excitedly got my line back in the water.

Two minutes later I ripped into another fish. This one was heavier yet, with no desire to come off the bottom of the lake. With this caliber of walleye, playing the fish becomes very important. You have to check your drag to make sure that if the fish makes a run, it'll peel line easily enough so as not to break the monofilament tether between the rod and the walleye's jaws. Even still, an experienced fisher person will follow the fish down, maintaining a good level of medium tension without putting undue pressure on the fish.

As this one got near the surface, my eyes bulged, and my heart thumped like a drum. I was into a different class of fish here, and while I was casually talking to the camera during the fight, I got intensely serious as I drew my net.

Just as I swooped that magnificent walleye, the hook popped out, and I grabbed the fish and swung it out of the net straight into the camera's face to show off a toad of a 25-inch fish. I was thinking to myself "This is it, man! These are the fish that are going to make my video! The fish that are going to make my business for next year!" Again, I played with the fish for a few seconds, got some good camera shots, and released it into the water.

Certainly, I wanted to catch more, but this had already been so epic, and I knew how amazing this video was going to be. The sun was really starting to fall, and I was down to perhaps ten minutes of daylight now lest I want to try loading my boat by myself in the dark. "One more good fish," I thought to myself as I set my phone on the edge of my boat again, camera on and prepared, confident I would get another bite.

I got in three or four good rips of my bait before it stopped completely dead. And then I felt the head shakes of a fish on the end of the rod. I looked to the camera, fish on my line, and said, "It's crazy when the bite is this good that I can just set the camera down and just know I'll get another good bite!"

The fish felt about like the rest, and I guessed it in the 23-to-25-inch range. But then as I got it closer to the boat, it really started to lean on me. The boat was sitting as still as an obedient young boy getting a haircut, not even needing a trolling motor or anchor to maintain position as pristinely calm as Lake Sakakawea was at sundown.

I got my money's worth out of that fish as it shook and dove over and over again. It was dead weight one second then lunging down or sideways the next. With each chaotic thump of my rod tip, I begged for the hooks to stay pinned. Rip jigging baits are heavy, larger ones near a full ounce, giving a strong walleye momentum to throw it each time it whips its mouth back and forth like a dog playing tug of war.

It was all on camera. Watching the film again later, I was having a ball of a time, laughing hysterically, and a psychologist not knowing what I was doing might have thought I was in need of services.

Again, at the moment of truth, I assumed a deadly seriousness as I reached for my net. The fish was much bigger than I expected. I rolled the thing into the net, and for lack of a better turn of phrase, completely lost my shit on camera. And then off camera. I slapped the side of the boat in ecstasy, hard enough for my phone to fall.

Shit! Had I just lost all of my fish footage? Not to mention whatever other important stuff might be on my phone?

Glancing out my peripheral, however, I noticed the phone simply fell straight forward and remained on the side of the boat. After a near heart attack, I propped it back up and continued filming.

It was such a gorgeous fish, strong with broad shoulders, beautiful scales, and typical Dakota-style walleye colors of green and yellow hues, twenty-seven and one quarter inches per my measurement. Now *that* was my money fish! All those 22-25 inchers became nothing more than supporting-cast gravy to a true trophy-caliber hog! Again, all on camera.

I got a beautiful release shot of that fish. I didn't think about the setting at the time, but my boat had spun just perfectly to have the sunset in the background as I dumped the fish back to its home. With its flared dorsal fin against that backdrop, it looked like Godzilla diving into the ocean. Walleyes, in fact, are often referred to as "gravel lizards."

I took a minute just to breathe it all in—the scenery, the fresh air, the epic events that just transpired. Then I had to finish the race.

I still had three miles back to the east boat ramp in Deepwater Bay, about as far back in there as a boat can go. Navigating there in the dark is no sure thing. I drove as fast as I could and as carefully as I could as the sun waved goodnight behind me.

Once a meandering creek before the building of the dam, the bay was now a sprawling piece of water, but not all of it deep enough to float a boat, especially with the lower water levels customary in the fall. As you get back further into the bay, there are plenty of low water spots and islands, sometimes submerged and sometimes dry, not to mention rocks and trees. It's a bit like driving a boat through a Formula One race at night but without the street lights.

It was probably the fastest I've ever loaded a boat in my life. I sat there in the parking lot all by myself, Jeep running, boat on trailer, now fully able to relax. I had just had the best day of fishing of my entire life, or at least the best three hours. It was certainly the best solo fishing I'd ever experienced.

I didn't even fish the next day. This seems insane looking back on it, especially since the next day boasted gorgeous fall weather and could've been just as epic, but all I could think about was getting the video online. After five hours of editing and a little bit more uploading, she was live. I had my master-piece, but beyond that a new level of resolve to hang in there when fishing was tough and embrace the suckage of the weather because, even though it isn't always, it can at times be so rewarding.

Perhaps the hardest aspect of guiding I have learned is keeping clients engaged when things are slow. The more confi-dent I can be—without lies or bluster—the more present clients will be to notice that bite after two hours of boredom and not miss a big opportunity. Projecting confidence you don't have is phony, and everyone will see right through it. Projecting from an abundant well of experience, however, can make or break a client's trip.

I didn't have to keep fishing that fall. I had no clients, and perhaps that video wasn't even as important as I made it out to be. But I knew that grinding it out for positive reinforcement was the biggest investment I could make in myself and my business. It's these behind-the-scenes sessions that take a person to the next level and give them an edge on the competition.

It's completely possible I got lucky that day, but I also knew what was out there and kept after it until I got it. I could now tell clients, with complete sincerity, that if we just stay the course, we'll get 'em. The confirmation was huge and paid great dividends the following season.

ONE GOOD BREAK

THERE'S a certain excitement that comes along with starting a new business venture. Not only is it novel but, ideally, you're following dreams that motivate and bring out your best work. This is a very welcome shot of adrenaline, because you need something to offset what could be crippling fear of financial uncertainty. If the excitement and motivation exceed the fear, you have a shot at being successful. Sounds like something you'd hear at a motivational seminar, anyway.

I had entertained ideas of getting part-time work during the winter to give myself more of a financial cushion. Then I remembered Brandon, SoulCycle, and my uncle's words. I had to go full on and put everything I had into it at the outset to give myself the best shot, no leaning on alternatives. I was fortunate my previous career and current financial situation gave me the opportunity to spend one if not two full years doing it right.

My first off-season was supposed to consist of grassroots marketing, promotional videos, and eventually face-to-face efforts through fishing and outdoors expos. Unfortunately, a viral pandemic was brewing that was about to shake everyone's world.

I had intentions of doing three expos, potentially four, before the coronavirus became a household news event. Thankfully, I was able to make the first two work in January and mid-February before the pandemic radically altered everyone's pace of life. I met a lot of fisher people, handed out a lot of cards and flyers, and got quite a few contacts to boost my prospective client list, learning a lot about the business along the way. And then the world was put on pause.

I'm not good at doing nothing, and I'm terrible at waiting. Besides, those are the last things anyone should be doing when starting a business. A guy ought to be out there hustling! It was like waking up on Christmas morning and seeing that pile of presents under a tree, and then your parents say to you, "Actually, why don't we just open them in April? Actually, we don't know if April's any good either. Let's just put a hold on this indefinitely and see how things shake out?"

Indefinitely. What a scary fucking word. What if I wait indefinitely and then comes April, May, June, and we're still not allowed to fish? Or even leave the state? Or everyone just panics and cancels all the trips? I need to do something! But I can't do anything. What do I do?

Well, I did still need a more permanent form of lodging in North Dakota. I had decided to focus my efforts on what had become my favorite fishery, Lake Sakakawea, so long as I could find a place to setup basecamp.

March was almost over, and being stuck in my house gave me way too much time to think. I was attempting to work on my laptop, tinkering with social media and web marketing, but my mind was stuck elsewhere. I'd been waiting many weeks for a decision from the Three Affiliated Tribes, the Mandan, Hidatsa, and Arikara Nations.

I was trying to work out a deal to swap guided trips for lodging at a casino in New Town, North Dakota. The manager of the marina was all for it, as he'd been wanting a fishing guide at his disposal for casino patrons, but the Three Affiliated Tribes, which runs the casino, had the ultimate call as to whether or not they're willing to forgo cabin rent to add a fishing guide to their list of amenities.

Even if I weren't in the start-up phase, guiding is not a highly lucrative business. Having to pay monthly rent while I stay up there and also continue my mortgage in Iowa would certainly make things extremely tight. Sure, a day of fishing has value, but trading that instead of cash would certainly help me out. And, theoretically, they would be lining me up with trips I wouldn't have gotten anyway, so I get more client exposure with less cash outflow.

Each time I called, there seemed to be a reason why the board meeting was delayed again. Such is everyone's life right now with COVID-19 hanging over us all like a big coffee stain on our collective calendars. I'm not really sure what I expected their decision to be, but I struggled coming up with reasons they wouldn't side with the manager of the marina. Besides, he said they used to put up other employees in the cabins for the summer as well, so I don't see why this wouldn't work.

Ding! New email. It was from the marina manager. The Three Affiliated Tribes voted "No." Well, shit.

Now what was I going to do? I had probably put too much hope in this idea and not enough into other possibilities. Then again, there aren't a lot of other partnership options on Lake Sakakawea, and I was pretty sure I'd checked all of them.

Though it wouldn't make my finances pretty, I decided I simply needed to find a place to rent to make it through this first full season. It would cut into my savings, but I needed to get that first year on the books to make this dream a reality. Hopefully then I could meet some people and make some connections, maybe work some other deal out for the following year.

Somewhat disappointed by the news yet also a little excited to finally have a task to do during the sanity-stealing solitude of quarantine, I started sending emails out to all the real estate agents I could find near Lake Sakakawea. I was open to almost anything. An apartment, a small house, a cabin, even a super small property I could buy on the cheap instead of rent would have to be considered.

Again, I waited. I'm not good at it, but what choice did I have? Thankfully, this time it was only two days instead of two months before I had a lead to work with. It was not what I expected, and certainly not one of the four things I had just listed as acceptable considerations. It was an option I didn't know even existed.

The response came from a real estate agent in Garrison, North Dakota. Turns out he was also an insurance salesman. And on the board of economic development for the town. I'm not entirely sure what it is he didn't do up there.

He introduced himself as Mike and proceeded to tell me about his background with the board of economic development. As luck would have it, they had put together an incentive program for fishing guides to bring more of them into town and give Garrison's economy a little shot in the arm. Typically, these incentives are paid out in vouchers redeemable at local businesses, but given I needed residence, and he was a real estate agent, he proposed to find me a place to stay and use the incentives to offset my cost of lodging.

I never imagined I would come across something like this, especially by simply emailing a bunch of real estate agents after essentially throwing darts at the Google search on my computer screen. If this offer was real, it would be such a huge break for my guide service. Was it real or was he just a bullshitter?

As his email continued, he wrote, "Just to be clear, I'm not a bullshitter," which meant he either was one or he was sincerely worried about sounding like one. Perhaps he was worried I thought the offer sounded too good to be true (it crossed my mind). Or maybe he told a lot of fibs as a child and had to spend the last few decades making up for them. Whatever the case, my intuition told me he was not, in fact, a bullshitter. Or maybe I was just too eager for help and to make this operation work. Nevertheless, I continued talking with him.

I responded with interest, and he responded with a copy of the guide incentive program. All right, they had a document, another level of legitimacy. Then he said I would need to write a proposal letter to the board talking about myself and my business and explaining how I could help the town. This due diligence continued to grow my comfort level. Although I had hoped I wouldn't need to fill out any more job applications after starting my own business, I was willing to make this exception.

Now armed with a decent contact list from my recent fishing expos, as well as a website, Facebook page, and YouTube channel, I sent off what I had. A few days later he informed me the board was impressed and was willing to move forward if I wanted to. I did.

All I had to do was advertise my business as being based in Garrison. Alrighty then! And with that, my business officially had a home. A month later, it *officially* had a boat.

It was a momentous occasion symbolized by the rather benign act of mailing an envelope. That little package contained the registration for the boat Dad and I owned, marked with a couple faintly-recognizable chicken scratchings confirming it now belonged to Bloemendaal Guide Service, LLC, a business entity solely owned by yours truly. It was a bitter-sweet moment approaching Dad about the buyout—this joint ownership was one of the finer excerpts from my life—but I was on a good path now, and he was all in on the idea.

"I knew this day would come; just didn't realize it would be this soon!"

Besides, it's not as if we still wouldn't have epic fishing adventures together; he'd just be riding in my boat next time around.

I had originally planned on arriving in Garrison mid-April, but the pandemic pushed that out to the evening of May 6. Mike told me to call when I was close to town for further directions and he would show up and hand me my keys. My residence was an apartment building on the second floor of the hardware store on Main Street, and, as it turned out, Mike's real estate and insurance office was right across the alley. As I pulled up between the two buildings, the no-bullshitter himself walked over to greet me.

"You can park yer rig right there. We set up an outlet there for ya to plug yer boat in."

I backed up the boat, shut off my car engine, and came out to formally meet the man who helped make this entire season possible for me.

"Boy, you just got a weekender boat there, eh?"

Did he expect a yacht?

"I'd shake yer hand, but ya know how it is. It's just diff'rent times right now, Brett."

"No worries, I totally understand."

He gave me a quick overview of my place, his office, and pointed out a few things on main street before handing over the keys.

"If you ever need anything at all, you just let me know."

I must've heard that twenty times over the next few months. He then drove off to spend the rest of the night with his family and his beagles.

As I carried my first of many loads into the building and up the stairwell, something about the heavy metal door, the dimly lit and exposed lightbulb without any fixture, the old wooden steps, and the painted cinderblock walls reminded me of the hallways in my old high school building. That old school had character and charm, but I only had the privilege of knowing it freshman year before we were moved to a newer facility for my last three.

The apartment itself had a retro, 1960s decor complete with evergreen-colored kitchen chairs, laminate table and counter-tops, and off-white wallpaper with burnt-orange floral prints. It smelled like a giant spice rack. I could think of worse smells.

Rotting corpses may have made me question my decision, but I could handle almost anything else just to be where I was and about to do the thing.

The bedroom had more cinderblock walls but was coated in white paint with a bunch of empty space, a bed, and a nightstand. It felt much more functional without any attention to aesthetics. My only concern was how comfortable the bed would be. I laid down for one minute and rose satisfied. The place was simple and dated, but it was just what I needed. After hauling the next ten loads of my belongings up the stairs, I slept.

A few days later there was an issue with the toilet, I don't remember exactly what, but it was something beyond the usual flapper and float switch issues an amateur could fix. I texted Mike, and he relayed the message to my landlord, Gary, the owner of the hardware store and my new apartment.

Later that day, Gary showed up in a mask, pleasant as can be, with a new float switch and flapper kit. Upon realizing there was more to the issue—evidently, I failed to properly communicate this—he said he'd have to call in someone else. We eventually got to talking outside the building, and he took off his mask. He could've been a twin brother to my Aunt Pixie, Grandpa Bloemendaal's youngest surviving sister. What better way for a new town to feel like home than a visual reminder of family?

Since Mike and Gary both worked either in my building or a five-year-old's stone throw from it, I had the fortune of making chit chat with them numerous times, and they did everything they could, within reason of a pandemic, to welcome me.

Eventually it was time to get down to business. My biggest challenge ahead of me was getting to know the east end of the lake. Yes, I was still guiding on Lake Sakakawea, but that isn't very specific when you consider the whole of it is one hundred and eighty miles by main channel from dam to dam. The downstream portion of the reservoir runs mostly west to east with a slight southern bent, and Garrison is almost all the way east. You can see the dam from town.

Based on the incentive agreement, I had to reside in Garrison, but I could fish wherever I wanted. Still, it would be nice to have a comfort level with the water immediately close to me. Many of my familiar fishing spots from past years were forty-five minutes to an hour drive, which would eat into profits and time. I tried to play a balancing act. Days I fished by myself, I made it a point to learn out east. If I had clients and didn't yet feel comfortable, we went west. For the entire year I would feel more confident in my old areas, but slowly the scales evened out.

By the end of May, clients finally started arriving as the pandemic receded to a degree and the weather warmed, making open-water fishing more enjoyable for the average fisher person. I enjoyed fifty-two days over the season with paid clients and another twenty with family and friends. I didn't know what to expect with two huge variables, it being my first full season and me attempting it during a pandemic, but it was starting well enough to keep me in the business.

Some clients cancelled, but others came who wouldn't have otherwise. A few had planned trips to Canada but then diverted to Sakakawea when international borders closed. I had a handful of clients from California and Florida who decided to purchase RVs and travel the country rather than stay in their house or a hotel. Any business selling recreation vehicles was fortunate to have been part of a unique bull market within a broader recession given how badly people craved outlets from quarantine.

For as much change as I had gone through, daily life was starting to settle into something very comfortable and very rewarding. I was running my business, in my element, and enjoying life until a rough September and a shitty social media experience.

CRISIS IN CONFIDENCE

THERE'S ALWAYS a bull market somewhere. It's a phrase used in reference to the stock market and popularized further by Jim Cramer, host of his own TV show, *Mad Money*. If you've never watched, he's a former hedge fund manager trying to educate the everyday investor in stock picking with his high energy antics and a gimmicky soundboard full of buttons he smashes to play sound effects emphasizing his points like "BUY BUY BUY!" for a good stock he liked or "Wha whahhh" for a stock that just got slammed by bad news.

He also happens to be an investment genius. I've never known anyone who could keep the financials of so many companies in his short-term working memory at one time and recall them so quickly on the spot. Lest you think it's only because he has a scripted show, you should watch him do his Lighting Round. I may have soured some on the investment industry in general, but I never soured on Cramer. I have a soft spot for people who are so singularly dedicated to their craft and/or purpose.

The phrase is quite true, by the way. Even in the worst of times, when the economy is falling apart and the stock market is being trashed, someone somewhere is benefiting from it all or continuing to do well in spite of poor business conditions. Case in point: RV and boat sales during a pandemic. Likewise, I was trying to find my niche as a business to best position myself as a relatively new guide as well as one attempting to navigate a pandemic economy.

One could also steal the phrase and tweak it a little bit to apply to fishing more specifically: "There's always a hot bite somewhere." Certainly, there are times when it's harder to catch fish than usual, but somewhere there are feeding fish, and if a boat has found them, they can probably catch them.

When fisher people say "the bite is on," this typically indicates conditions are ripe for feeding and a large percentage of the fish are all feeding at the same time in different locations. In other words, your likelihood of running into a hungry fish and catching it is much higher. Likewise, when the bite is "off," conditions are not ideal for fish to feed, though there may be a few here and there that do eat, so your likelihood of running into biting fish is much lower, yet never impossible.

When you consider a lake as big as Sakakawea, with over 360,000 acres of water, this can work for you or against you. With that much water and millions of walleye swimming in it, there are going to be a few biters roaming around. When the bite is tough, however, there is a hell of a lot of ground to cover to find the few active ones.

Outside of the immediate post-spawn period, I can't think of a tougher time to catch walleyes than the transition between late summer and fall. As the seasons transition, so do the fish, setting up on different locations more advantageous to the changing weather conditions. They don't all move at the same time, however, so they become more scattered. A fisher person's friend is consistency in order to pattern fish, and transition by definition is not consistent. Likewise, fish distracted by their own migration sometimes seem less inclined to worry about food.

Intellectually, I know all of this, yet it never gets any less frustrating year after year trying to catch fish when they just don't want to bite or you can't find them at all. You try to remind yourself of all of these things, but after a couple weeks' worth of struggles, you start to worry you've lost the touch. Or you start to wonder if there's something wrong with the lake. You start to ask yourself, "Do I even know how the hell to fish at all?" It's like watching Tiger Woods go out and shoot an 81 on the PGA Tour and all the talking heads rushing to be the first to proclaim he is finally washed up.

Then, for one day, maybe two, you stumble on a good pod of hungry fish. "I found it back!" you think to yourself. Or you think perhaps finally the bite has picked up, the fall bite is here, the post-spawn bite is here; whatever it is, the fish are on again. But then it's back to a few more days of struggle. What likely happened for that day or two is, even though the odds were against you, you found the one little bull market out there on the lake.

I was in the midst of these struggles mid-September, but I was doing a pretty good job of reminding myself of the conditions. Most days we would catch two or three walleyes, some days a few better if we were lucky. The National Walleye Tour (NWT) was set to hold an event in Garrison at the end of that week, and I was curious to see how well the best pros in the world could do on our fishery during such a tough bite.

I was honestly thinking it would be a struggle and the weights of the fish entered would be lower than we were used to seeing on Sakakawea. Actually, in a somewhat sick and silly way, the narcissistic part of my subconscious was actually *hoping* they would struggle and that that would make me feel a little better.

By and large, it definitely was tougher than it would have been during a better time of the year, but there were still over a hundred boats of professional walleye fisherman out there for those two days, so someone was probably bound to find 'em.

I had the good fortune of being able to chauffeur one of the cameramen and witness some of the action firsthand. I also helped with the weigh-in, sorting entered fish between those likely to die, which went into an ice chest to be cleaned, and those likely to live, which went to a release tank.

As interesting as the process was, it was probably not very good for my fragile ego. To be fair, there were a lot of boats, driven by professional fisherman, mind you, bringing in zero or maybe one or two fish on the day. But there were also plenty who found their bull market and brought in their limit of very sizable fish. And when you add it all up and start looking at all of these massive walleyes in water tanks and freezer chests, you start to ask yourself, "What the hell have I been doing? Do I even know how to fish?"

Never mind the day-one leader of the tournament, also a local angler and fellow fishing guide at Sakakawea, managed only one entered fish out of his five allowed on day two. All I could think about were those piles and piles of big fish swimming out there the whole time, the ones I was now seeing and unsuccessfully attempted to catch for the better part of two weeks.

Shortly thereafter I went out fishing with another local, a man who, in fact, had fished as a co-angler in the tournament, a partner to a different pro each day. I was testing out new boats and wanted to take his for a spin, and we decided to try catching a few fish along the way. As a sidenote, we only caught two walleyes on this day as well. At one point while the fishing was slow—which was nearly all day, but we had accepted our plight now—chatting took over as the main event, eventually leading to this:

"Were you aware that you were the topic of recent social media conversation?" he asked.

"I can't say that I am, do tell."

He let me scroll through his phone to see the latest gossip.

The first thing that struck me, before I even began reading, was the number of comments made at the bottom of the post. Certainly, the topic was engaging plenty of people aside from just the poster. And then I read the content.

Generally speaking, the dude was upset and disappointed the

town of Garrison had "hired" me as a fishing guide when there were plenty of other local guides he felt were better and more capable. He said he had "heard" I was not making clients happy and was struggling to catch them limits of fish. At one point he scribed I was "running around the lake like a kid chasing an ice cream truck" and asking everybody else where they found fish instead of finding my own.

He then ended his editorial with a list of names of those he considered to be better fishing guides who people should call instead of me and signed off with "Asking for a friend, sorry not sorry."

Okay then.

First of all, I'm not sure what the motivation was for him writing this. I do know he is involved in the local fishing and hunting industry in North Dakota, but I've never met the guy. I don't know if he was sincerely concerned the town could do better. I don't know if he simply was friendly with the other guys he mentioned and wanted to boost their business. I don't know if he perhaps had aspirations of guiding himself and this was more of a personal matter for him.

The second note worth pointing out is the fact that Garrison didn't "hire" anyone. The economic development group has a guide incentive program any fishing or hunting guide can take advantage of so long as they fill out the paper-work and advertise as being based in Garrison. As I read further through the comments, I noticed a few other guides I recog-nized who commented to this point and said it simply didn't work for their business and that they had passed on the opportunity.

Toward the end of the comments, one of the directors of the economic development group actually stepped in to defend their program (and indirectly me), explaining how the incentive program works and how I was the only one who applied for it. She also mentioned that if anyone else would like to apply, she could forward information to them same as she had done for me, and if anyone had any issues with their program, they could contact her personally.

The part of the story I will remember most is the ice cream truck comment. I also found it so appropriate that one of the commenters was the lady who runs the Ye Olde Malt Shop in town. She chimed in how she quite liked me being around as I brought in a lot of business with my clients looking to enjoy ice cream after a hot fishing day. I also found it rather amusing to learn the ice cream lady was the poster's own grandmother.

The general consensus seemed to be most people were surprised and disappointed at his comments. They felt them to be inaccurate and uncalled for. In fact, he actually wound up losing some of his sponsors over the ordeal, not to mention the confidence and opinion of his own grandmother. By and large, I felt comfortable with the support of the community as a whole and the economic development group who had helped me base my business out of their town. This helped immensely because the worst-case scenario obviously would've been the opposite, leaving me fighting a huge uphill battle in the future to continue building my business in the area.

Even still, the comments stung and remained with me for quite some time, not necessarily because I thought they were going to have a business impact but because parts of them had connected with some of the doubts I was already having during the recent tough stretch of fishing, especially out on the east end. Maybe I didn't know what the hell I was doing. Maybe I wasn't ready for this. Maybe I didn't deserve their incentives (even though it was their choice and they would offer them to anyone bringing business to town).

And then I thought, how else is someone supposed to start a business like this? What would anyone else have done? If he was disappointed that they gave incentives to somebody from out of town with less experience than other folks, then he should've asked those guides if they were even interested in the program. He also should've gotten his facts straight about who had actually done what here; as I said before, I wasn't hired by anyone, and it wasn't the town of Garrison involved but rather its economic development group.

Obviously, I ask other people about fishing anytime I get a chance. We can only learn so much by ourselves, and I value constant improvement. I like to think we can learn throughout our entire lives; just because I'm continuing to learn doesn't mean I'm not ready to teach. Besides, we actually have a small network of guides within which we regularly share information to help each other get on and stay on fish as well as take clients out when any of us already has a full schedule.

As far as the ice cream truck comment, I sure as hell am not going to sit on one spot with clients for eight hours when we're not catching a damn thing. Reservoir walleye fishing can often times mean hitting many different spots in a day simply because of how frequently they move. If anything, I would say some of the guys I know move even more frequently and try more spots than I do. I've actually been trying to be *more* mobile as a goal rather than grinding out spots for too long. It *is* rather like chasing an ice cream truck, but it's fish you're trying to chase down instead.

It was the perfectly wrong comment at the perfectly wrong time, catching me at a period of weakness. But it got me to think more about what I consider a fishing guide to be. More specifically, it got me thinking about what kind of fishing guide *I* wanted to be.

I want the total client experience to come first. For many people, simply being on the lake in a boat with a chance is more than they would've had otherwise. If they feel they were able to do something they wouldn't have been able to do on their own, then we added value.

I also want to teach them something. I want them to learn how to catch the fish by themselves. I want them to learn how to feel the bite. I want them to learn how and when to set the hook and how to fight the fish up to the boat and get it in the net.

Some may want to learn a new technique. Some may want to learn something about boating. Some may want to learn something about how to use electronics to find fish when they're on their own. If they learned something, then we accomplished something.

What I hope to offer is an ongoing knowledge of and passion for the activity, something that will endure with them long past their last day in my boat. When they're standing on the shore of the lake, river, or pond near their house and catch great fish, hopefully they can look back on something we did together during their trip and understand how it applied to the last fish they caught.

I want it to be about more than simply taking home the maximum number of fish the law will legally allow them to consume. Certainly, catching fish is the focal point, and if we are doing it right, hopefully we'll catch plenty. But I don't want them to be observers of a fishing machine pulling in fish just so they can take them home if they had very little to do with the catching process. If our boat catches fifteen and another boat has twenty-two, it doesn't inherently imply our day was a failure.

I want my clients to be the judge as to how well I'm doing my job. I don't know how much truth there is to the fact one angry person heard some of my clients were disappointed, and perhaps it doesn't matter. Certainly not every day is going to be a wild success, but I hope over time the experience is positive more days than not.

In essence, I want to be the guy who teaches a person to fish rather than just catching them fish.

I never expected this to be easy. Fisher people, especially those who's fish catching literally puts food on the table for their families, are an infamously tight-lipped bunch. If you ask many of them where they caught their fish, they will often tell you something to the effect of "in the water" or "in the lip." Some of them may take you out to their honey holes but blindfold you first and swear you to secrecy.

A few of them, however, are more helpful than I ever imagined, and for this I am beyond grateful. Anyone who ever accomplished something worthwhile had help from others along the way.

Still, this one disgruntled person specifically tried to sabotage my business and send clients elsewhere simply because, well . . . I don't know exactly. As if it weren't already hard enough to build confidence in your first full season starting your own business. Perhaps in the long run this is just what I needed. In a situation where all the stars were seeming to align as I charted my course from dream to reality, perhaps I needed to be reminded that being authentic still takes effort. And being authentic will always wind up pissing off someone else who doesn't appreciate you being you.

Which is okay, cause I'm here, and I'm not going anywhere. Sorry, not sorry.

LIGHTER SIDE OF FISHING

SURE, the process of throwing away a financially reliable career in investments and setting out on your own to become a fishing guide is a gut check full of emotional highs and lows, including loads of stress and adversity. But it's also a lot of fun. Sometimes it's even funny. After all, that's a big part of the reason why I chose this path: I thought it would be a lot of fun. I haven't yet acquired the encyclopedia of fish stories a thirty-year vet may have, but I do have a decent enough set list for one good chapter.

After my second official guiding trip, I went out by myself the following day to scout out some new spots. It was a comfortable early summer day with bluebird skies and a light breeze, perfect conditions, and a busy boat ramp proved it. When it was my turn, I backed my boat into the water, motored off the trailer, and slipped the free end of the rope over one of the dock posts. Then I jumped out of the boat, got into my vehicle, and sped off to my parking spot so as not to prolong anyone else's launch.

As I'm jogging back to the dock, one of the other boaters politely informs me, "Hey, your boat is drifting away!" Sure enough, once I peeked around the corner of the brush that lined the shore, my boat emerged, twenty feet and counting from the dock as it continued drifting toward the middle of the bay. My face flushed and my heart rattled the inside of my rib cage. I yanked everything out of my pockets and set them down in a pile as carefully as I could without slowing down my forward motion. I ran into the water until it reached my breastbone and then paddled after my boat like a parent whose child was drowning. Soon I reached the starboard side and hoisted myself over the side rail and into cockpit, drenching the carpet with about a gallon of the Missouri River water.

As I sheepishly idled back to the dock, one of the other boaters offered to hand me my belongings. As I reached out, soaking wet from head to toe, they handed them over and calmly said, "You know, we could've taken you out to your boat for you."

It had all happened so fast. I just reacted without thinking. Looking around after the fact, there must've been four or five boats within a hundred yards of the dock waiting to board passengers. Any one of them could've quite easily given me a ride to my boat, sparing me some level of embarrassment and wet clothing.

I spent the next three hours using my windshield as a drying rack and fishing pretty hopelessly in the back of the bay, almost too ashamed to do anything else and not wanting to leave until my clothes dried. All I was wearing was a pair of rain pants with nothing underneath. At least it was a warm, sunny day.

As I fished, I did a little post mortem on the events. The slipknot which was slipped over the cleat on the boat had come loose, and the rope was left hanging on the dock post by the knot on the other end. I then started to flash back to the previous day when one of my clients was untying the end of the knot fixed to the boat, at which point I had told him it was a slipknot and he could just loosen it. At that point he had retied it but perhaps not securely enough to hold the pressure of a boat drifting in the wind a day later. Of course, I forgot to check his work. Guide tip number eighty-six: check your own knots.

Fast forward about a year, and I'm still crossing my fingers, worried one of these days I'm going to have a client go over the side rail. The water can get a little rough on Sakakawea, and I had been prepping my mind for the inevitable man-overboard drill.

It was early August, but it was also early morning and a day after an unusual summer cold front. We were all wearing rain gear and warm layers as we prepared to fish at our second spot of the day. Thankfully, we got out of the wind a little bit there, and then the wind almost died down altogether. We were jigging the end of a point, so I had decided to use the GPS anchor on my trolling motor to hold our position, though we probably didn't even need that as we were sitting almost completely still.

My clients that day were a lovely couple, both sixty-some years of age. He did most of the rambling, and she often had to remind him what he'd forgotten to say or do. They had that forty-years-of-marriage chemistry, the kind where they act like they can't stand each other but totally belong together. They'd brought their own boat along but wanted a guide to show them around before they set out on their own.

The husband knew fishing, and he wasn't shy talking about it. But he was the sort of guy who could get distracted by his own story and forget what he was doing. His wife and I were in the back of the boat, and he was sitting up on the bow resting his haunches on a cooler. It was turning into a beautiful day as the sun had finally peeked through the clouds, and we were patiently waiting for our first bite.

As he's talking to me about a certain jig he wants to try, he reaches forward and grabs a tacklebox to extract one. Leaning back toward the cooler, he overshoots his mark and lands on the back of the cooler, prompting it to roll backward and send him somersaulting backward over the side of the boat and into the water.

My heart shot so far up my throat I could feel my pulse in my teeth. His entry was damn near a perfect dive, and he plummeted out of sight. I leapt up to the front of the boat where he entered, ready to play lifeguard if need be. Knowing how difficult swimming can be with all of that gear, I don't think I exhaled until I started to see water displacing around him as he finally rose toward the surface. I'm sure he was even happier than I to finally take a breath of air again. As soon as he grabbed onto the side of the boat, he was in jolly good spirits about the whole thing, already smiling and laughing.

In the process he had lost a good pair of sunglasses, but somehow his hearing aids stayed put. I helped pull him into the boat, and he began stripping off clothing and drying himself. At that point, as I finally looked around the boat, his wife appeared not to have moved or reacted throughout the whole ordeal, arms and legs still crossed, properly holding a fishing rod in her dominant hand. With a straight face and sunglasses, she deadpanned, "I can't believe you've done that now twice this year, honey."

Anyone can fall in the water, but it takes a damn good man to laugh at himself afterward. Twice. As his clothes dried, we proceeded to catch a nice limit of walleyes.

During a particularly tough early-season bite and by far my worst outing of the year, one of the women in the boat asked if she could put her deli meat on the hook as bait. I was in no position to argue that day. An hour later, as we headed back to the dock, she reeled up her line with a fully intact piece of sliced ham. We caught one bass that day; it was on a night crawler.

On one of the better bites of the season, we had a limit of fish over eighteen inches in ninety minutes, apparently the exact amount of time for the husband to feel comfortable enough in my company to constantly fart and blame it on his wife. He wasn't fooling anyone, and she caught the majority of our fish.

A favorite repeat client of mine typically enjoys a pipe and a nap in the afternoon. I enjoy swerving the boat just enough to almost make him fall off his chair.

During an outing with one of my nieces, we learned it is customary, and even necessary, to slap the fish after you catch them to make sure they're alive.

"Ya gotta slap it! That's how ya know it's alive. I get ta slap 'em all!"

I suspect the Game and Fish disagrees.

On a particularly windy day at Sakakawea with my dad, we were drifting across a sunken island, and I was fishing two different rods as permitted by law in North Dakota. One was pulling a bottom bouncer with a spinner and live bait, the other a crankbait. At one point the crankbait rod, which I had stuck in a rod holder, snagged up on a tree. I set my other rod down in a different rod holder, grab the snagged rod, and two seconds later the other rod became snagged as well.

At this point I was holding two fishing rods, both with snags. Fortunately, the one in my left hand released from its snag, so I dropped it down in the boat between my legs to focus on the other. Two seconds after I dropped it, it hung up on another snag, and the rod jumped up over the side rail of the boat and into the water.

With one rod still in my right hand, I lunged into the water with my left, trying to grab the rod just out of my reach as it slowly sank below the surface. When I realized it was completely gone and was overcome with ARE-YOU-FREAKING-KIDDING-ME rage, I threw an adult version of a mini temper tantrum and slapped the water twice with my hand.

After getting this out of my system, I looked to the front of the boat where my dad was sitting peacefully, just watching.

"Something wrong?"

I had no good response. I did, however, later learn that the sunken island we were fishing on was once covered in a forest of lively cottonwood trees.

A year later I was fishing with my uncle Fred at Devils Lake in North Dakota. This time it was a balmy, calm day in October, and we were vertically jigging with both live bait and artificial jigging baits, just dropping them down to the bottom and popping them up a few inches in hopes to attract a fish's attention. For some reason, Fred kept wanting to "cast" his bait without reeling up or letting out any more line, kind of old school, bamboo-rod-style casting.

On about his fifth attempt at this, perhaps a little under the influence at this point, he flung everything, line, rod, and reel, twenty feet out from the boat and watched it sink out of sight. The funny thing is none of this looked awkward; it was all one fluid, graceful motion. There were no last-minute lunges or grasps, almost as if he was doing exactly what he intended to until the delayed shock registered on his face. He turned to me wide-eyed and cried, "Dude! I'm so sorry, man!"

"It's okay," I said. "It's my dad's rod."

A few years ago, I was fishing with Dad, Brando, and Tyler at Waubay Lake in South Dakota. We had a pretty hot bite going in the last couple hours of daylight that October, which I assume made the following all the more difficult. Tyler became even more stoic than normal stoic Tyler. He was holding a couple things in. Eventually he let one out by telling us that he had to go. You know, GO. Like NOW!

Being miles from a boat ramp and in a hurry, we found the nearest beach with a nice side-lying tree for a bench, handed him the cleanest hand towel we could find in the glove box, and wished him the best of luck. Yes, a hand towel. No, we did not have toilet paper on the boat. I'm sure it was all a bit traumatic for my brother, so I won't rehash too many details here, and I suppose you are okay with that as well.

After the fact, however, I couldn't let him escape this situation without a nickname. We already often called him T-Dawg, and we had recently watched the sketch from *Key & Peele* where they announce football player names before an all-star game. Tyler had come up with a pretty good one that weekend, Dijon Mustaford. Inspired by that and recent events, I dubbed him T-Dawg McDeuceford from Waubay State University. He wasn't thrilled, but he always appreciates solid comedy. He finally opened up and told his wife the story this past Christmas in front of the family, so here's hoping he doesn't sue me for putting it in a book!

Immediately after this event, I began looking for karma over my shoulder so frequently I developed a crick in my neck. I just knew one of those days I was going to find myself locked and loaded with nowhere to shoot. One year went by, then two, then three. With each day I got on and off the water safely, I considered it a victory, but the inevitability started to haunt me, much like death in the *Final Destination* movies. I would drive to the boat ramp each morning silently wondering, "Is this it? Is it today?"

This past September I was preparing for some solo fishing at Douglas Bay near Garrison. I prefer to use the old ramp back in the northwest finger, the one that doesn't have a park, a bathroom, or even a portalet. For whatever reason, as I walked past the bathroom on the way out of my apartment, I saw one fresh roll of toilet paper staring at me out of my peripheral, almost crying out "Are you sure you don't need me?!" "Okay, just in case," I said aloud as I grabbed it and walked to my vehicle.

Whether premonition or self-fulfilling prophecy, halfway to the boat ramp I could feel it. As I reached the launch and exited my vehicle, I faked ignorance. I went through my prelaunch checklist, of course making sure to release the tiedown straps at the back of the boat as I'd never forget again. I shouldn't have launched that boat. Then again, it also seems unlikely, in hindsight, that I would've made it fifteen minutes back to town either.

I immediately ran the boat as far back into the bay and out of sight as I could and answered nature's call. Karma won, but at least I had toilet paper.

This journey has turned out to be the best decision I ever made for myself. Every story I tell, every flickering image I relive, and every photo or video I take in with my eyes fills my soul to the brim. For every naysayer there are a hundred supporters. For every tough moment, there are another ten great ones. As long as the scales tip in that direction, I'm happier and lighter every day.

The dull white walls and ghostly gray lighting of the corporate office have been replaced by the vibrant colors of the beautiful Lake Sakakawea landscape, splashed by the lifeblood of the Missouri River and the golden rays of a life-giving sun. The cubicle has been traded in for a fishing vessel, the ultimate open floor plan. Monotonous mouse clicks have morphed into a chorus of birdsong and rolling waves with the welcomed disruption of fish breaking water and clients shouting in joy.

I still get tired after a long day of fishing, but it's a good tired, the feeling of having put in effort so worthwhile you sleep like a baby and pop up the next morning refreshed, barely able to wait till you drop the first line in the water. It's the feeling I used to get before seeing the water for the first time after a long drive with Dad to "The River," the adventure of chasing down big fish and not knowing what's about to happen. And the most important part of it all hasn't necessarily been my fishing but the sharing with others.

There was a time when I would sit at my office desk wondering if I could make it through the day. I'd stand in line at lunch not knowing how much longer I could go without sitting; the longer the line, the more potent the anxiety. I didn't know whether I'd stay conscious during my meal. I had many friends watch me barely able to stay upright during our conversation. It wasn't that long ago, but somehow it feels even more distant than my fishing memories of childhood.

I don't know exactly what was going on inside my hunk of flesh. I don't know how this change helped make it better, if it healed my body, my mind, or my soul or all above the above. I don't much care either. I'm home now, and that's all that matters.

DREAMING OF TV FISHING

AT DIFFERENT TIMES DURING CHILDHOOD, I dreamt of being the starting quarterback for the San Francisco 49ers. I wasn't big enough, strong enough, or fast enough, but I thought I'd work harder and outsmart everyone. I wound up a tight end in high school for a team that ran the ball ninety-nine percent of the time, essentially making me a small, blocking lineman. Back troubles then cut my career short my junior year; no Superbowl rings for me. Then again, Tom Brady is still playing, and he's older than I am, so you never know.

In high school or early college, I might have chosen to pursue the PGA Tour if I had more talent than it takes to play varsity for a Division III university. In my mid-twenties, I thought a standup comedian would be a pretty sweet gig. I thought about getting into health coaching as wellness became more popular, since I was well read on the subject anyway.

This all turned out to be either wishful thinking or transient phases.

Around the same time my heart was stuck in a San Francisco daydream, I obsessively consumed TV fishing shows. I loved Bill Dance swiveling in his pedestal seat while fighting a squirrely bass, sometimes losing his signature Tennessee Volunteers cap in the water, at times even falling in himself during an awkward turn or a misstep at the dock. He was either a terribly clumsy dude or they eventually started scripting it into shows; it happened much too frequently for coincidence.

I was beside myself watching Jimmy Houston plant his puckered lips on a slimy largemouth bass for the first time. Then, of course, I had to go catch one myself to try it. It was easier than catching girls at my age, anyway. And who doesn't love listening to Al Linder yammer on in his signature accent and cadence explaining how they're catching those big "donkey" walleyes? Or listening to Babe Winkelman set up the tale of his last fishing adventure from his cozy cabin setting, fireplace and mounted fish in view just behind?

I was always amazed at how easy it looked. Within a half-hour show, they would catch more and bigger fish than I had in my entire life up to the tender age of, I don't know, probably eight or ten. Dad stepped in as the voice of reason, same as he had done when rudely crumbling my blissfully ignorant love of professional wrestling.

"They could be fishing for multiple days and are only showing the good parts on TV."

Assuming this was the case—and I now know it is—they were still catching those fish. Well, at least most or some of them were.

There was just something so cool about capturing a fishing moment on video, a moment by no means certain to happen. You don't know what you're going to catch, but you do have to fill a show. I just assumed it was a testament to their superior skills, and to some degree it is. I figured they could probably come to the little ponds, rivers, and lakes where I lived and catch all the fish I thought I should be catching. It never occurred to me there just might not be many good fish in those places.

What a life it would be, traveling the country, fishing all of the best lakes and rivers it had to offer, and making TV shows! This is what I wanted to do. I first started pondering the idea shortly after college, I believe, after one of my own amateur attempts actually came together quite well.

When we were little, my mom owned a handheld video camera, and my brother and I, sometimes with the help of my friends, would make silly home videos. I must say, we weren't bad at it either, for our age and the resources at our disposal. There was some level of production quality; we did have a wardrobe of costumes to draw from thanks to Goodwill and my mom's packrat tendencies, and we entertained family and friends numerous times over.

One particular weekend, Brandon and I were both visiting Mom as young adults, and we all got to talking about those home videos as we often do over dinner. We were planning to do a little fishing the next morning anyway, and I asked Mom if she still had the camera, which she did. Brando and I then began scripting out our first ever fishing show.

We called it "Fishing with Fred." It was clearly meant to be silly, as we didn't expect the fishing to be all that good. Fred was also a made-up character and never made an appearance in the show; we thought the irony and mystery would add another level of humor as we asked ourselves at the end, "Who is Fred anyway?" My name was Bill, a campy homage to Mr. Dance, and I can't say I remember my brother's character. We were basically spoofing the entire concept we loved because it was the only way we thought we could get anything out of it.

We shot the video at our step-grandparents' farm pond, which was stocked with bluegills, bass, perch, and a few walleyes. Brandon actually made an intro with his guitar, covering the theme song to *King of the Hill*. We even had some pretty good B-roll of us driving out to the pond with some twangy country music and a mug of coffee as we mused about our upcoming fishing day. Then we started casting some lines and filming.

We could not believe how well things came together. We were getting plenty of fish on camera, and we were even getting the strikes and the hooksets. The bass were on a pretty good topwater bite, and topwater strikes are amazing on camera since you can see the fish exploding on the water's surface to take the bait. At one point I was casting a frog lure and actually caught a live bullfrog, which turned into a scene we infamously dubbed "frog on frog action." We still made it funny and silly, but we actually had legit fishing action as well.

If I've had one beef with the fishing industry, especially the television aspect, it would be the false sense of certainty projected by some of these personalities. Obviously, editing would gloss over dead time and mishaps, but the tips and tricks revealed often misrepresented their effectiveness. They gave the impression fish were completely predictable, you just had to use their tips—and sometimes the tackle they shame-lessly pushed—in order to have amazing fishing day in and day out. Much of the content was marketing disguised as education.

As I started to get questions about fish behavior and location during my first official year as a guide, it shook my confidence; I felt a bit fraudulent to not have all the answers. I think most people expect guides to have all the answers. But the truth of the matter is that fish are not perfectly predictable. They have certain behavioral tendencies, and if you study them enough and fish for them enough, you become better at putting the odds in your favor, but there are no guarantees.

Fish are their own beings making their own decisions, and part of the game is simply trial and error. Even something that worked yesterday or last year under similar conditions isn't guar-anteed to work again today. And sometimes, believe it or not, the fish may do things that seem a little bit irrational. Or perhaps there is just a new variable we humans failed to see.

This is what I find so refreshing about the modern-day YouTube fishing boom. It's much more in touch with reality. Take one hugely popular channel, *Uncut Angling*, for instance. The whole premise, and it implies as much in the name, is to show everything, good or bad, to give you an idea of what fishing can really be like. And, trust me, they are some great anglers, but the show doesn't always come off as perfect.

There's an inherent struggle in the business, though, whether making video content or guiding clients. On the one hand, you want to prove your expertise and show potential clients or viewers you know what you're doing. On the other hand, you don't want to give them a false sense of predictability and then have them be disappointed with the outcome. The more we can be transparent about reality, the better off we all are in the long run. If you're good enough, eventually reality will look better than the average reality for most fisher people.

I now have my own YouTube fishing channel—Bloemendaal Fishing, by the way, in case you're interested and willing to forgive shameless plugs—and it's been about as much fun as I expected it would be all these years. If I get days without clients, I set up the camera and get as much on film as I can to put together a show. I try to get good camera angles, good audio, and good fish catches for intriguing content, but I also want to balance it with a sense of reality. I don't want it so polished anyone who fishes with me after watching a video leaves disappointed. I believe in the appeal of authenticity.

I want viewers to see how much I enjoy fishing and think they could enjoy it as well. I want them to see how sometimes I both struggle and succeed depending on the day. I want to be myself, which more often than not can be a little goofy and silly. I get more intense when the fishing is tougher, but I try not to take myself too seriously on the water. It's supposed to be fun, and I do everything I can to at least put us in a position to let the fish speak for themselves.

Early in my first full season in Garrison, North Dakota, I ran into a fellow at the fish cleaning station by the name of Randy. He was a short, stocky guy wearing a big old bucket hat cleaning fish in front of his much taller co-fishermen, his dad and brother. I was scouting that day and kept a couple of fish for myself to clean for dinner.

"Hey, you're Brett Bloemendaal, aren't you?"

"Ha! Why yes, I am," I said, a little shocked a stranger recognized me in Garrison. "You must have seen my article in the newspaper when they introduced me as a new local guide?"

"No, I actually watch your YouTube channel. I was studying it to figure out how to make a fishing video."

Say what now? Poor sucker. Anyway, we talked a little more while cleaning our respective catches, and then I asked him if he wanted to go fishing sometime. And so, we did.

Randy is an extremely likable and friendly human being. He has a wide surfer-bro smile he stole from California on his way back to North Dakota and a penchant for firm handshakes. He's a grade school teacher in Garrison but also does some extensive videography on the side. Eventually he got more into fishing, and the two interests married themselves and had an obsession baby.

We've had a lot of fun fishing and filming together. I brought more of the fishing expertise to the mix, and he was clearly more dedicated to getting everything on film than I have ever been. In fact, I'm not sure I ever saw the guy fish without at least one camera blinking red somewhere; for him it's pointless if not on record.

He loves pouring over the film and editing it into something watchable; at best I only like the process and mostly tolerate it. It's a means to an end for me. We made a pretty good team that season. I'm anticipating even better things next year.

He quickly became one of the first two friends I made in town. It was just another piece of the puzzle coming together to make this whole dream a reality for me. And it all started just by putting out some half-ass amateur fishing video, him finding and watching it, and then randomly running into each other at a fish cleaning station.

It's been interesting fishing with lots of other really good anglers as I've gotten into this business. After having idolized some of the big names as a kid, I now know some of the reality behind the scenes. Much like other things in life, it's just doing a few things a little better than everybody else that makes them who they are. They aren't magic, and most of them aren't doing things any other fisherman couldn't do; they just do it more often and pay attention to the details.

I had the good fortune in the fall of 2020 to film with the crew of *Fishing the Midwest* when they did a show at Lake Sakakawea. Again, they are a really accomplished group of people, and they put together a really good production, but they aren't magic. They're just people like you and me. Over two days of filming, we had our struggles, in part because their schedule brought them there a little early for the fall bite, but when it was done, we put together a pretty sweet production. I was thrilled to be part of it. As often happens during a day of fishing, stories were told. One in particular really stuck with me.

The crew was about to do a fishing show at a location I will not name. When they arrived at the lodge, they found a stringer of walleyes tied to the launch dock. They asked the lodge manager if he had a good day of fishing, and he replied, "Yeah, I went ahead and caught some fish for you beforehand!"

"What do you mean?" this TV fisherman replied. "We prefer to catch our own fish."

"Oh! Well, the last guy who came and filmed here had me catch the fish for him."

I won't mention any names, but the story taught me everything I don't want to be in this business and reaffirmed how some of those fishing "gods" I looked up to as a kid might not be quite so amazing after all. At best, they're regular people who work hard at their craft and spend a lot of time on the water. At worst, someone else catches their fish. TV magic.

FULL CIRCLE

It was July 3RD, the first of four days of fishing with Dad and Brando, and the first time I had both of them on the boat together since I started the guide service full-time. I was excited but not anxious.

I used to fish as if every day was my last on the water, like it was the one open look I got in a middle school basketball game during my obligatory two minutes of playing time. Everything rested on one shot. This approach can be helpful in terms of focus, but it's destructive to the extent it adds unnecessary pressure. And it's simply an exhausting way to be. It's fear of missing out rather than just being present and showing up with your best. It's literally anxiety.

I can see some of my old ways still living in my brother (and, trust me, they're never completely exorcised either). It's easy to forgive him, though, because I know what it's like to only have a few days rather than six months to get everything out of a fishing trip. Too much pressure gets placed on every decision. Where should we launch the boat? Should we go north or south? Which spot should we try first? Shallow or deep? Live bait or artificial? The bite is usually best in the morning hours, so we better make sure we hit all our best spots before noon.

The best fishing was still taking place in some of the major bays on the lake, and I'd been focusing on two prominent ones as of late, Deepwater Bay and Douglas Bay. I suggested we try Douglas the first day and Deepwater the second. Since our slate was still clean, and everyone was optimistic at the start of the trip, there were no objections.

As we reached the ramp and began preparing the boat, Dad studied the surroundings with a critical eye. Perhaps he was internally questioning our plan to fish in this bay rather than the main lake. Most trips in his heyday were peak summer when all the good fish move out to bigger water. If he was, he never put it into words. After backing the boat into the water, I revved up the Mercury and the growl of the engine lit Dad's fire.

"God, I missed that sound!"

The tone of Dad's voice shot a bolt of adrenaline right through my spine.

Fishing was quite productive in the morning. We got plenty of fish and some healthy ones too, no monsters but a couple near twenty-three inches. A hot and calm afternoon quieted the place down, but after a solid morning, it was hard to complain for day one.

Day two was the Fourth of July, and the lake was extremely crowded with eager boaters, both fisher people and some joy riders for the holiday. And it was hot. And calm. And the fishing was terrible. We managed one decent walleye in five hours and decided to leave the water and get out of the heat, which was now over ninety degrees. Then my brother's anxiety set in.

He could feel the trip slipping away; he was just doing the math. After the first two days, we basically had half a day of good fishing and the rest was pretty unproductive. I could see his head spinning, and out came the ideas.

"We need to be on the water by sunrise or we're going to miss it. And we have to go deeper. The fish must be deeper. We didn't catch anything in eight-to-fifteen feet. It's too hot, they've moved out already."

I sat and listened, watching my old reflection in his panicked face. And then I smiled.

"We just need to go fish. Today was an anomaly. It was hot and calm and super busy, but the fish are still there. It was hot above the water, but the temperature below the surface isn't warm enough yet to drive 'em out. But I'll compromise with you, we can still go out earlier if that makes you more comfortable."

The next day we went back to Deepwater. We were on the water by eight o'clock in the morning, and with overcast skies and a little chop, the bite was pretty good right out of the gate. We started putting together a pretty good bag of eating fish, and then I picked up a 23-inch walleye for a catch-and-release photo. Later that afternoon, Brandon tied his personal best with a 26-inch walleye in fourteen feet of water. We never fished deeper than fifteen feet that day. Trip made, and still one day to go.

Brandon was right in pushing us out earlier in the day. While the fish still hadn't moved out deeper for the summer, they had started biting earlier now that they were passed those spring days of waiting for warmth. Our best action was certainly the first hour of the day. Sometimes fishing is a fickle contradiction; you have to stick to your guns and be willing to change, all at the same time. I stuck to my guns on depth and location, Brandon got us open to fishing earlier. Both landed us on some really nice fish.

After cleaning our catch and filling our bellies with fish tacos, we sat around discussing where to launch for their final run. Technically the pressure was off to some extent after a great day on the water, but you always want to try to make the next day great too. I also really wanted to get Dad a big fish before they left for home. Evidently, he was thinking the same thing. When I opened up the floor for discussion, Dad looked at me and said, "What's the best chance at getting me a big old piggy?"

I contemplated silently for a few moments and then replied, "Probably Douglas Bay."

"Douglas Bay it is, then."

Again, we were on the water early, which was easier to accomplish given the proximity of Douglas Bay to Garrison. Our first spot came up empty, and after a couple small bites on our second spot, I started to notice what I thought were nice fish marks way up near shore on my side-imaging screen. Brandon decided to cast up there while Dad and I were trolling our spinners, and on his third or fourth cast he hooked into a nice 23-inch 'eye sitting up in probably five feet of water.

We then put the spinners away and got out the jigging rods, proceeding to catch probably a dozen more fish up there shallow, but none of them came close to matching the size of the first one. In fact, I don't think any of them made it into the livewell, as most were thirteen or fourteen inches in length. As the sun continued to rise, the shallow bite started to fade out, and we decided to go looking once again.

We returned to our best spot from day one, but it didn't have the same magic. We threw a couple two or three decent ones in the livewell, and then went back into search mode. The next two spots came up empty as well. It appeared as though the fish weren't going to make it easy for us to finish with a bang.

We tried fishing a little deeper on some spots as we got closer to the afternoon, more in the 18-to-25-foot range, but still only a few more eater-sized fish. Had I been taking out a standard client group, I might have stuck it out on some of these spots, but I know my dad too well. And he knows that I know. It's all about one big bite at this point. The big fish were still up shallower, we just had to find the spot.

I decided to try a couple of extended underwater points productive for me in the past. Within the last week some of the weed lines had started to grow up along these points as well, and the weed edge was coming out to where the water depths were fourteen or fifteen feet. I told them we were going to troll right through the weed edge, pulling spinners and night crawlers through the cabbage. It was sparse enough to be only a minor inconvenience, but it was thick enough to hold bait and big predators looking for a meal.

It takes a lot of trust and confidence to troll straight through this sort of vegetation. You don't go more than a few seconds without one of the weeds grabbing your hooks and loading up the rod. It takes a lot of patience and attention to sort through the weed pulls and fish bites, to continuously clean off fouled lines. But I had a ton of confidence there could be a couple big fish in there, and we stuck with it.

Dad was sitting in his familiar position from my childhood. Though he was not running the boat this time, he was occupying the front seat up in the bow, working his bottom bouncer and spinner just like the good old days. He no longer had that Jean-Claude Van Damme from *Hard Target* perm, but the salt-and-pepper hair and whiskers had a presence about them as well, that of a wily, grizzled veteran.

After a few minutes, I saw his rod bend out of my periphery. Dad rarely gets stressed or anxious; he treats most everything in life with the exact importance it deserves. I could tell he was giving this moment all the appropriate attention, whether the obstruction be a leafy green plant or a large Sakakawea walleye. At the last second, he seemed to have concluded the interference was plant not fish as he started to pull back to free his line until it pulled back the other direction and he quickly accelerated his pullback, set the hooks into the fish, and yelled "Be on! Oh, please be on!"

It's a phrase I've heard many times before, a phrase I've said many times myself. You get so close to messing up a good bite, and you're afraid you were a split second late in pulling the trigger. You can feel the fish still shaking on the end of the rod, but you don't know how securely it's hooked. As the fish takes you for a ride, you just hope, maybe pray, those hooks made a good connection.

After a couple of runs and dives, we can tell it's a great fish. I so badly want those hooks to hold.

As it gets near the surface, we can see the eyes and the white-tipped tail, the dead giveaways of a walleye. Years ago, this might've been the sort of situation in which I would freeze in the presence of my father. I would relinquish control to him, waiting for him to tell me what to do. A few years ago, in fact, not wanting to wait for him, I jumped too early with the net and knocked off a nice fish of his at Devils Lake. But this was a different time, and we were different people. I'm the captain now. In the blink of an eye, that fish was in a net and lying in my dad's lap. And my *God* it was gorgeous, a long, svelte female leaned up after having dropped her eggs and hungry to put the pounds back on. It had a darker, more golden tint than some in the reservoir, perhaps a function of residing in shallower weed beds as its primary habitat. What a predator.

After a short video and a couple of pictures, Dad goes to measure the fish. Resting on the tape, you could only slide one of Dad's grey whiskers between the tip of its tail and the 27-inch mark. I started thinking back to all those times in our childhood when Dad held up a large fish and proclaimed, "Now *that* is a Pierre walleye!" I don't think any of those fish were this long. *That* was a Sakakawea walleye!

It had been a wild ride the last six years. After not fishing for way too long, then buying a boat together, one I figured would simply serve as a means for more quality time with Dad, I had no idea I would eventually use it to start my own business. To work as hard as I had toward this goal and learn as much as I had during these last few life-changing years, seeing Dad with this fish and that old smile may have been the most fulfilling part of the entire journey. Like he always says when someone catches that one big photo fish, "Trip made."

It's not a lake house, but maybe it's enough. He never got his Tyee either, but the following season would bring a brand-new, fiberglass Lund Pro-V into the arsenal of Bloemendaal Guide Service, one step above the Tyee, and Dad forever has a VIP family discount to enjoy that boat and every other one we wind up using from here till our last day on the water. I don't want to take for granted a single second of any of our future trips, no matter how many there may be. He's given me so much, and I don't know if I can ever fully reciprocate, but I'll be damned if I won't try. And maybe, just maybe, the lake house will materialize someday.

As Dad is set to release the fish, I'm using my phone as a video camera to capture the moment. To our knowledge, it's the largest walleye he's ever caught. He cradles the fish in the water, coaxing it to return back to its home.

"Come on, schweetie," he says, talking to the fish like one of his tender, young granddaughters. "Come on, schweetie."

Within a few seconds, it comes to life, vigorously whipping its tail to propel itself back down to the weedy depths from which he borrowed it.

"Woo-hoo-hoo! *That* was a pig!" Dad exclaims with as much jubilation as I can remember him showing over a fish in years. He begins to turn away, then hesitates, looking back as if he remembered he has unfinished business. He points to the camera and starts to speak in his best twangy, fishy accent.

"Thanks, Bloemendaal *Guide* Service!"

Thank *you*, Dad.

And thanks to Brando too. The journey wasn't easy—nor is it over—but the answer was simple: cast a line. I figured the rest out along the way.

PLEASE POST A REVIEW

If you enjoyed this book, or even if you didn't, I would sincerely appreciate you taking the time to post an honest review. As authors, we want nothing more than to reach as many eyes as we possibly can. The best way to do that in our modern, digital world is for our readers to leave a digital trail. The more reviews a book gets, the more attention it gets, and the greater the likelihood it will be discovered. If you enjoyed it, please don't keep it to yourself. Give it a rating. Write words if you're so moved. Even once sentence will do.

Thanks for being you.

WANT MORE FROM THE AUTHOR?

You can follow Brett's business as a fishing guide, watch his YouTube channel, or connect with him on social media:

Bloemendaalfishing.com
Bertbetterman.com
Bloemendaal Guide Service on Facebook
Brett Bloemendaal on Facebook
Bloemendaal Fishing on YouTube
Bloemendaal Fishing on Instagram

ABOUT THE AUTHOR

Brett Bloemendaal is an author of memoir, essay, and other nonfiction, including his Bert Betterman blog. He left his fourteen-year career as an investment professional to become a full-time fishing guide on Lake Sakakawea in North Dakota, where he spends half the year. He spends his winters in Iowa focusing on writing and other content creation, including his YouTube channel for his fishing business.

ACKNOWLEDGEMENTS

In no particular order:

To Mom and Dad for bringing me into this world and doing your best in your own unique way. Also for indulging me in my questions and being willing characters in my story.

To my siblings . . . Tyler and Brandon for being amazing brothers and sources of inspiration, Tyler for showing me how to just "do the thing," and Brandon reminding us all to "cast a line." To Teryn for being another writer in the family and making me feel like less of an oddball creature. To Taylor for being my first of four wonderful sisters and showing me how great our complex family could be. To Nikki for making me feel like an incredibly old older brother and Ashley for being a great sister and first making me an uncle.

Also to Taylor and Brandon for effectively being sensitivity consultants on family matters for the contents of this book.

To my uncle Bevan for encouraging my writing and sending that airplane email all those years ago that provided me with my first strong example of living authentically.

To my best college friends—who also remain my best friends to this day—for providing pivotal moments in my journey and in the book: Brett Selk, Jeremy Cook, Brad Beyer, and Eric Johansen.

To Alina for first being a great coworker, then a great coworker friend, and now simply a great friend. No hugs required.

To all of my critique partners and beta readers of various degrees for being brave enough to read some pretty rough stuff and help me turn it into something better: Danielle Vandehaar, Jessica Cahill, Brandon Bloemendaal, Bevan Bloemendaal, Taylor Schlichting, Jami Kitchel, Alina Lindgren, Mike Burton, Sharon Burton, Patrick Molony, Kelly Van De Walle, and Eric Johansen. And thanks to Danielle for essentially being a developmental editor disguised as a beta reader; your above-and-beyond efforts got more out of me than I knew was possible and also gave me the confidence that I was writing something worth sharing.

To my amazing editor, Shire Brown, for being professional and honest and again squeezing more out of me than I thought existed and polishing the prose to ready it for the world.

To Randy Belisle for being part of my fishing and vlogging journey and taking the most amazing photograph that wound up gracing the cover. And, of course, to Laura Boyle for taking Randy's photo and shaping it into such a wonderful end-product cover.

To everyone in Garrison, North Dakota, who made me feel at home and helped me get my guide service going: Mike Matteson, Gary Larsen, McKaila Behles, and Lindsay Bofenkamp.

To my buddy on the Big Muddy, Kent Yancey, for being the closest thing I had to a mentor in the fish guiding business. I would have wound up here somehow, but you made it so much easier and made the experience much richer. You didn't have to do any of the things you did, but I'm grateful for all of them.

To my wonderful clients for fishing with me and—for some of them—allowing me to include their experiences in this book. The stories added another level that I couldn't have achieved without it.

To Sarah for encouraging me to follow my heart.

To everyone else who was involved in my journey or this book in any way, shape, or form. I don't have enough space for all the names, but if this sentence made you wonder, "Does he mean me?" I probably do.